Frustration of Shame

Frustration of Shame

In Defense of America's Teachers

Bruce J. Gevirtzman

ROWMAN & LITTLEFIELD
Lanham • Boulder • New York • London

Published by Rowman & Littlefield
A wholly owned subsidiary of The Rowman & Littlefield Publishing Group, Inc.
4501 Forbes Boulevard, Suite 200, Lanham, Maryland 20706
www.rowman.com

Unit A, Whitacre Mews, 26-34 Stannary Street, London SE11 4AB

Copyright © 2017 by Bruce J. Gevirtzman

All rights reserved. No part of this book may be reproduced in any form or by any electronic or mechanical means, including information storage and retrieval systems, without written permission from the publisher, except by a reviewer who may quote passages in a review.

British Library Cataloguing in Publication Information Available

Library of Congress Cataloging-in-Publication Data Available

ISBN 978-1-4758-2870-2 (cloth : alk. paper)
ISBN 978-1-4758-2871-9 (pbk. : alk. paper)
ISBN 978-1-4758-2872-6 (electronic)

∞ ™ The paper used in this publication meets the minimum requirements of American National Standard for Information Sciences Permanence of Paper for Printed Library Materials, ANSI/NISO Z39.48-1992.

Printed in the United States of America

Contents

Preface — vii
Acknowledgments — ix
Introduction: A Bum Rap — xi

1 The Myths of Superman — 1
2 Frustration of Shame — 17
3 It Ain't the Coal Mines — 29
4 A Straw Man Named Tenure — 43
5 Not a Teacher's Friend — 55
6 Good Teachers, Bad Advocates — 71
7 Feeding the Hand That Bites You — 83
8 One Size Does Not Fit All — 95
9 Making the Grade — 109
10 Teachers Are People, Too — 121
11 The Naked Emperor — 135
12 Forbidden Territory — 153

Index — 167
About the Author — 171

Preface

Restorative Justice is the last straw.

Last spring, when I first heard that term, I knew I needed to write this book.

Teachers are getting the screw. With Restorative Justice, the screws have been tightened.

A policy of "Restorative Justice," as it has been termed by the Los Angeles Unified School District, is the school board's way of telling its teachers to go to hell: student defiance, no matter how severe, along with streams of vulgarities and obscenities, no matter how offensive, is no longer punishable by suspension or expulsion. Classroom teachers have been in tears over this new policy. When a child is blatantly defiant, disruptive, or destructive of a class's environment, there is practically nothing a teacher can do to regain control of her classroom.

How would you like to be a teacher under *those* conditions?

Yet another spear has been thrown into the heart of America's teachers.

The powerlessness of teachers to control their own destinies may eventually kill off public education as we know it. The shame felt by teachers—and the ultimate frustration brought about by that shame—may prevent our best and brightest from entering our profession.

My investigation of America's schools has produced this text, one that admits to the flaws in the system yet defends the overall integrity and hard work of the men and women who are the nucleus of public education. Teachers catch the heat. They get blamed and shamed. But teachers are not the problem. Not by a long shot.

We are not Finland or Japan or Sweden. We are the most heterogeneous, multicultural, diversified nation on the planet. And while diversity may be good for a lot of different reasons, it presents special, inconceivable problems for America's teachers.

Acknowledgments

My thanks to the people, including friends and family, I spoke with and poked for answers to some of my questions. Many of them raised issues I hadn't previously thought about. A special thanks to my teenage children, who were occasionally willing to give me some peace and quiet at home so I could complete the manuscript. If an idea or concept does not make sense to you, it is probably my son's or daughter's fault for distracting me.

My wife, Janis, an A-grade teacher, sometimes pointed out the flaws of teachers that were *not* defensible, and I thank her for doing that. It helped to make my ideas more credible.

Introduction

A Bum Rap

"What are you, Daddy?"

"Huh?"

"What *are* you?"

"What do you mean?"

"Are you an American, a man, or a daddy . . . ?"

"What?"

"My social studies teacher wants to know how you see yourself *first*. Pick one."

"I am all those things, Dude."

"But what are you *first*?"

"I'm a *teacher*," I answered my nine-year-old son, who now looked disappointed.

After teaching high school for thirty-seven years, I retired. I was suddenly a stay-at-home, old Daddy. Even though I should have selected from the choices he gave me, I told my son I was a *teacher*. If my wife had been in the room when our son asked me that question, my answer would have been different: I definitely would have said *husband*.

My life has been dedicated to helping other educators, teaching our children, placating their parents, and making our schools better. We teachers have made a lot of mistakes; *I* have made a lot of mistakes: maybe a startling revelation coming from the author of a book, which has, as its primary purpose, the defense of teachers. But trust me: my confessions give my arguments in favor of teachers more credibility, my research more authenticity. My honesty should make you chuckle during those moments you are not cringing. You might even chuckle and cringe at the same time.

An example of our shortsightedness is that we rarely defend ourselves to politicians, community, and parents. Maybe we've forgotten how to do that. Maybe we've lost our willingness to do that. Teaching is tough; it takes its toll. Maybe we want to curl up into a ball and take our last professional breath.

Everyone knows somebody *else* who has an excuse for every deficiency in his character and for every lousy choice he has made in his life. He backed his car into a tree: blame the booze he consumed. She forgot to pay the electric bill: blame the diversions with her children. He lost his job: blame the unreasonable supervisor at work. The list of rationalizations can be endless. Sometimes those excuses cross the border of the ridiculous: they become cannon fodder for neighborhood chatter and water cooler gossip.

Benjamin Franklin, who deplored the habit of excuse making, wrote, "He that is good for making excuses is seldom good for anything else." Or, to say it another way: excuses may let you off the hook for something you may have inadvertently done, but it doesn't change anything. The result stays the same. If you made a bonehead move, the move was *bonehead*, no matter what the reason for it.

This is not to argue that excuses are never helpful. Excuses might explain a behavior or a condition. But they do not justify it. The reason my son doesn't do well in math is he doesn't get enough sleep at night. *There*. In case you want to know the culprit behind my son's ignorance in math class: it is his lack of sleep.

But a lack of sleep is his fault (or my fault as the lazy, neglectful parent who doesn't make sure his kid sleeps enough at night). We can't fix this until we parents acknowledge our part in allowing it to occur.

Let's stop making excuses. Let's stop our denial. Let's stop the constant parade of finger-pointing and blame baiting. In other words, let's be real. The sole reason—the only reason—America's schools stink is the teachers in those schools. *The teachers stink*. If America's teachers didn't stink, everything in our schools would be hunky-dory.

Yeah, right, and I look a lot like George Clooney.

Teachers get a bum rap. They have become objects of ridicule, rationalization, and scorn. The scorn is new—at least, coming from parents and the general public. Teachers used to be held up on a pedestal. But not anymore: now they are viewed as a major reason why our children are doing so poorly in school.

Are educators the main culprits in the education crisis? Taking responsibility for their faults is crucial, and they must do so from the get-go:

1. Educators make poor decisions.

This applies to any profession. Sometimes people do the right thing; sometimes they do the wrong thing: Surgeons occasionally remove the healthy kidney. Carpenters don't properly bolt the main screw to the beam. Cops shoot an unarmed suspect. Nobody escapes short-term mediocrity in what they do for a living. Educators make a slew of mistakes: whom they hire, whom they fire, and what they prioritize. And money. Educators have made so many money mistakes that people have stopped counting or commenting. It's embarrassing. These mistakes have made people, inside and outside education, scratch their heads. Dumbfounded.

2. Educators keep changing their minds.

Trends, fads, and fashions abound. What's hot one minute is cold the next. Teachers, administrators, counselors, plant operators, facilitators, aides, workshop organizers, in-service presenters—*everybody* gets absolutely thrilled about a new concept . . . and a few years later, they reluctantly admit embarrassment for their previous support for that concept. At the very least, they shake their heads in bewilderment that someone turned them on to that malarkey in the first place. What was nothing short of the Second Coming has wound up on top of the trash heap. Sure, it's good for them to admit their mistakes. Sure, it's good for them to change and grow and adapt. But *those* bizarre ideas? *Really?*

3. Educators live in the past.

There's a big difference between being stubborn and being tenacious. Being *tenacious* is a good thing. It means you know you are right—at least, think you are right—and stand up for what you believe in. *Stubborn* means you know you are wrong—or suspect you are wrong—but stay by your faulty position anyway; in the process, you look like an imbecile.

Over the years, educators have *stubbornly* refused to release their time-honored faithfulness to overcrowded classrooms, destructive teacher-tenure polices, idiotic evaluation procedures, useless standardized testing, robotically structured school days, and unreasonable expectations that every kid will go to college (not *should* go or should have the *opportunity* to go—but *will* go).

Educators have supported policies that promote diversity over competence, and curriculum that emphasizes equality over excellence. Some of us dream about how we wish things *were*; others have embraced reality, the way things *are*. In either case, the resulting paralysis devastates our schools.

By the way, simply advocating more technology in the classroom and the conversion of those hapless standardized test forms into cool computer-generated modalities doesn't make an educator appear hip or mod; in fact, it makes him look like a total dimwit if he doesn't know what he's talking about.

4. *Educators line up to defend mediocrity.*

In the end, it is educators who control the trends in our schools. It is educators who decide where money is spent and how money is raised. Teachers and administrators often lock horns with each other; they also lock horns—though not as much—with parents, communities, and political leaders.

Ultimately, those closest to the classroom should have the final say. That they do not is gross negligence or flagrant ineptitude from those in charge. Our schools' leaders captain a ship that values diversity over excellence and equality over freedom. Educators have gone with diversity and equality for a long time now, forgetting the age-old philosophy that there is an enormous difference between guaranteeing the *opportunity* to get an education and guaranteeing an education—*period.*

You can lead a horse to water . . .

Educators relish the idea of siphoning millions of dollars from our thoroughbreds and divvying it up among a bunch of deadbeat horses. Everybody drinks from the same trough; but as the slow get a little faster, the fast get a little slower. Then they meet somewhere in the middle, and a philosophical higher ground is achieved. But to what end?

5. *Educators haven't figured out that silence is tantamount to tacit approval.*

It's *okay* to go after child molesters; in fact, it is good. It's wise to be skeptical of a teacher whose suspicious behavior would pique our concern, like the pods in *Invasion of the Body Snatchers*. Educators who go after their own for disgracing their profession give education a shot in the arm. Nobody is talking about a witch hunt. God forbid. But good old-fashioned common sense, decency, and courage go a long way toward preserving the integrity of those who follow the rules and do the right thing, day in and day out.

The leaders of teachers unions could use a course in situational ethics. They should remember what it was like when they first brought their children to school and how they felt as their own little girl disappeared into the classroom of a stranger they had met only five minutes ago.

Changes in our schools are needed. We can throw around terms like Common Core, process learning, cooperative grouping, international standards, community buy-in, and team teaching until we are the proverbial blue in the face.

Local school districts send teachers to workshops, in-services, and collaborative learning centers, paying millions of dollars for a recurring result: stagnation. Sometimes it is worse than stagnation—much worse: actual regression occurs. Educators become confused. The public becomes distrustful. And children, those whom educators are supposed to be all about, are *hurt*. Often they are hurt beyond repair.

Their shame drives educators to the excuse bank, while the public and their political leadership wind up at the blame distribution center. Educators claim that society is letting the kids down because parents are neglectful and the public doesn't care. The public argues that educators in general—and teachers in particular—are deficient for a variety of reasons, not the least of which is incompetence. Sometimes they claim it is even worse than incompetence, that teachers are driven by sinister agendas that use our children as their targets.

This scenario is depressing, the truth complicated. Many excellent teachers have been lumped with awful teachers—have been spoken about in the same breath, in the same tone, as terrible teachers. Those who know better, who wish to reform the system, to bring America's schools back, suffer from the frustration of knowing what to do, how to fix wrongs, how to mend ills, but must tussle with those who know nothing.

Our journey through this text brings to light what some people don't want you to know. Our revelations about America's teachers specify repairs; they step on some toes, too—shove a few faces into the dirt, and kick some big-time ass. America's teachers don't get off the hook, but blame is hurled where blame is justly due.

After the dust has settled, teachers may pointedly assess the job they have been doing through the wisdom of Muppets creator, Jim Henson: "[Kids] don't remember what you try to teach them. They remember what you are."

Through this lens, we focus on America's teachers.

Chapter One

The Myths of Superman

In his most memorable screen performance, the late actor Glenn Ford plays a rookie high school teacher. But not just any high school teacher: Glenn Ford stands tall among his teacher colleagues on the faculty of a troubled urban high school. In the 1955 drama *Blackboard Jungle*, Ford, abrasively labeled Mr. Daddy-o by the aspiring young thugs who sit in his classroom, plows through mazes of fists and bullets on his way to taming a few dozen surly urbanite teenagers.[1]

He pulls off miracles with those hooligans. Mr. Daddy-o doesn't die in the movie; he doesn't have sex with students, either. Because of his heroism, a young, smirking Sidney Poitier eventually abandons his wayward path. Even Daddy-o's wife begins to like and respect him again.

On many occasions, Hollywood has exalted America's teachers: *Blackboard Jungle's* Sidney Poitier was cast as an underdog teacher in 1967's *To Sir with Love*. Poitier plays a goat in *Blackboard Jungle*, and twelve years later he's on the screen cuffing around younger and testier goats, this time in London; or Michelle Pfeiffer's rendition (another English teacher, of course) of a sultry, smack-talking teacher in *Dangerous Minds*, a 1995 movie that proves female teachers can be tough, too, especially those who were in the Marine Crops. As long as she throws some Bob Dylan and Dylan Thomas her students' way, what's not to like?

Numerous other movies have done the same: venerated the role of a lone teacher in the disheveled, disoriented lives of her students. The more down the kid, the more up the teacher: the more fractured a child's life, the more glory for the teacher who rides into his life. *Glory* is defined by the scope of the rescue, and the quality of the teacher is measured by the enormity of the challenge she has met.[2]

Teachers all over America throw everything they have into their days' work, commit every fiber of their being into helping children. The sacrifices teachers make are colossal, sometimes firing signals to throngs of laymen that they are crazy for making such level of commitment.

As films like *Dangerous Minds* make their rounds, a myriad of seemingly forbidden questions arise. But are educators allowed to wander outside their boundaries of altruism and formally ask probing, provocative questions about issues that perplex them? Certain questions about this genre of films beg to be asked.

1. Where are the parents?

This is a disquieting first question, because a physical presence of the parents of troubled children is nonexistent. In educator-saves-kids-from-a-life-of-hell movies, the parents are seldom around. Sometimes they are given token representation in a film, either as sappy single mothers who haven't a clue as to how they wound up as single mothers, or as tough-talking workaholic fathers who haven't given their sons the time of day since they last chastised them for letting their hair grow too long. These films often indicate that the dads have been incarcerated: a hard truth in the neighborhood demographics customarily depicted in these utopian movies about teachers.

Parents are never seen. It's as though these kids materialized out of vapor and took their places on a movie set. The viewers know enough to disconnect the actors on the screen from the characters they depict, but lending some credence to that difference takes an effort. The self-rule of movie children—and television kids, too—is alarming. Parents never discipline, advise, or serve. *They simple are not there.* But Michelle Pfeiffer is there; she suffices, managing to transform worthless dust into gold dust.

Who drives down a metropolitan street, glances out the side window of her car at unsupervised young men loitering on the curb—apparently ready to shoot the first thing that looks at them cross-eyed—and thinks, "Hmm . . . now that's going to be trouble! Somebody's going to get killed! What those boys really need in their lives is an involved, energetic classroom literature teacher!"

The temptation to create *Wanted* posters to ring in these missing parents is immense. As movies about errant teenagers in filthy, dilapidated inner city schools drone on, most educators develop a sense of shame. Ready to hop on the nearest white horse and ride to the rescue, they forget about the improbability of disappearing parents comforting the lives of these needy children; it's as though the parents were never there in the first place, and somebody had to step in and do the job those parents should have done. Teachers, of course, wind up on the front lines.

These movies bring on more head-scratching reservations.

2. Why would a sane person want to teach in one of those schools?

In order to qualify for a teaching position, a candidate has to jump through hoops. As with most other professions, all this jumping presumes some pain along the way. For would-be teachers, there are notable differences from other professions, and the question, "Why would a sane person want to teach in one of *those* schools?" is more than just academic. And it often leads to befuddlement.

The answer may lie in an interpretation of the words *sane person*. Maybe a sane person would *not* become a teacher—at least not in this day and age, not during a time when children care more about Facebook than they do about a textbook. During an era when new technology has brought endless distractions upon students, it is understandable that educators fume with indignity when they are told that cell phones, iPads, and other digital appliances should be making their lives easier, not more difficult, and woe to those teachers who can't grasp that concept![3]

A *sane person* soon finds out that there are few teaching jobs available: thousands of education graduates pouring out of universities with no place to go, no way to get help to pay off their accumulated debts and to mollify their nagging, finger wagging "I told you so!" families and friends.

While viewing *Dangerous Minds* twenty years ago, America wasn't agonizing over present education dilemmas. Today, the inner city science teacher is not the only guy who has to worry about a gun-toting renegade who has fallen off his rocker; in fact, most school shootings occur in *suburban* neighborhoods.[4] A modern-day teacher scans his classroom for inattentive students who are surreptitiously peeking at their cell phones for a glimpse at their girlfriends' personal panorama *and* has to guard against the—albeit, slight—chance that a lunatic might barge through the front door with a pointed gun and busy trigger finger.

What *sane person* would want to deal with that, while having to put up with the snickering, scary adolescents Mr. Daddy-o encountered every morning? After watching Mr. Daddy-o and his science teacher colleague being beaten to a pulp by their students, one may consider turning off the movie; it's not hard to fathom teachers getting to the point where they consider turning off their *careers*.

Yet they hang in there, day in, day out, from crises to crises. From their first breaths in the morning to their last breaths in the evening, before they retire to their sweat-soaked beds where they encounter ritualistic nightmares, these fictional teachers have chosen their paths; and the seemingly fair, logical question, "Are these folks nuts—or what?" demands an actual answer.

In 1998, this author's brother-in-law received his credential to teach high school history. By *choice*—these kinds of choices hardly ever exist anymore—he found work at a dilapidated, rundown school in the center of the most economically disadvantaged section of Los Angeles. By 2000, he was done: finished, caput—his teaching career over. His grandiose dreams of becoming another Mr. Daddy-o were never realized.

Now an ATM repairman with severe bowel problems, he looks back with a shrug on his days in the bowels of Los Angeles. His desire to pursue his dreams and do something special with his life only brought him to his field of nightmares.

"I thought I could save the world," he observed.

But it took a small part of the world to save *him*. His family and friends, most of whom attended the same church as he, provided him comfort. Health crises, largely contributed to by his two-year stint in the center of the volcano, came close to killing him. The effects of chronic intestinal problems linger; so do lung ailments. Enduring consequences of frequent panic attacks from those bygone days still plague him.

It is a fair question: *Why would anybody want to become one of those teachers we see in those hero teacher movies?*

Here are a few hunches: the perennial satisfaction moviegoers see on the faces of the accomplished, successful teachers at the ends of these films is not the main reason Mr. Daddy-o would endure knifings, beatings, and threats to his wife. Sidney Poitier's "Sir" provides a hint in *To Sir with Love*. He contends that some people have it in them to give; others . . . choose only to take.[5]

Another important reason teachers take these jobs: they are often the only jobs available to them. From 2008 to 2013 there was a 74 percent drop in teacher hiring, with 78 percent fewer teachers retiring than in the previous three years.[6] Graduating from teacher-education schools and finding gainful employment as an educator is a depressing venture. Young people have become disillusioned. The National Education Association reports that college students are staying away in droves from education schools.[7]

Because of hiring freezes during the last several years, students are changing their minds about their futures. Declaring education as their major has become a joke on college campuses. People talk about others who are studying to become teachers like they used to talk about Uncle Ned's diagnosis of cancer. By the water cooler, in a *whisper*: "Have you heard about Ned? He . . . he. . . . I can't believe this; it's so sad. . . . He's in college to become a . . . *teacher*."

3. *How do teachers like Mr. Daddy-o always know how to say or do the right thing in order to reach those kids?*

Even Mr. Daddy-o doesn't always say or do the right thing. Those asphalt schools are a tough place to work. And suburban schools, especially those in the more upscale parts of town, are armed with never-ending armies of parents and lawyers who make sure teachers reach *their* kids—or else. But extortion doesn't guarantee success. Teachers—say this carefully—*are people, too*. They come with warts and pimples, just like other people do. They all don't look like Michelle Pfeiffer, although even Michelle had warts in *Dangerous Minds*. Those warts came in the form of her inexperience while dealing with children who made the thugs in *Lord of the Flies* look like the motivated, talented studs in *Glee*.[8]

Autonomy gives you the freedom to be more creative, more venturous: if you mess up, you have the flexibility to fix it; if you leave something out, you have the freedom to put it back in. Without autonomy, you are still quite capable of making mistakes. But it is more difficult to fix those mistakes because you may not have the power to fix them—at least, the way you want. Without independence, the pressures and stresses from the outside may cause you to rupture on the inside.

Today's teachers have lost their autonomy.

Ms. Johnson (*Dangerous Minds*), a former marine turned teacher, doesn't always know what to say or do. She experiments, learns by trial and error. Her mistakes glare in neon. But she has (the script gives her) the potential to edify the lives of her students and offer them what they need.

Not everyone is suited to Ms. Johnson's style. Not all teachers relish visiting their students' homes and confronting their parents. But Ms. Johnson has to take liberties, needs to circumvent crazy-ass rules that probably don't exist in the real world of education. She takes chances, sometimes with her life, that no sane teacher would have taken, unless prompted by a screenwriter's computer.

Ms. Johnson adapts to her students' pop culture tastes and shares some of her own tastes, often creating an uncomfortable atmosphere (which, of course, transmogrifies into a virtual love fest by the conclusion of the movie, despite the requisite tragedies that occur along the way). In short, this movie teacher learns how to be successful while on the job, but is guided by a carefully crafted script, with a core objective of getting moviegoers to buy more popcorn and come back for a second viewing of the film. She *has* to succeed; otherwise, the movie would tank.

4. Are these films' portrayals of students and teachers realistic?

Yes.

And no.

Hollywood scripts typically follow a formula. If the formula leads to unexplored territory, preview audiences are pulsed by the studios. Depending upon the results gained from the feedback of those audiences, the ending of the movie can be rewritten; the entire film can be rewritten, too.

The direction that most movies about teachers take is linked to the direction audiences *want* them to take. People don't walk away from *Dangerous Minds* and say, "Yeah, it was a pretty good movie, but she should have killed off a couple of kids. That would have made it better—more action." Or, "I wanted the teacher to die by the end of the movie. She was really annoying, and it would have been more realistic if the teacher croaked."

Film has become a medium for venting. Even more than television, because in television the rules and restrictions for content are so voluminous, while film is a vehicle for giving Hollywood's perception of society—or at least the way they would like society to look. When a movie, sometimes inadvertently, reveals truths that the kingpins in the celluloid industry do not want audiences to hear, protest speech (think *American Sniper*) runs amok. Longwinded, inappropriate sermons are presented at the Oscar ceremonies; if the politically correct line isn't fed to film audiences, blacklists emerge, tails spin, and heads roll.

Glenn Ford's Mr. Daddy-o is a laughingstock to sophisticated modern audiences. Michelle Pfeiffer's Ms. Johnson is hot by any standard or to any audience, but her teaching methods attract more than a fair amount of derision. Making sweet talk with hardcore gang members, trying to appeal to their softer, more sensitive sides, works only in the movies. And even then, it doesn't always work: at least, not for critics and a fair number of refined movie watchers.

Laughable is a word to describe the following plot lines and outcomes in movies having to do with teachers and schools:

- A teacher who dances in a strip joint at night shares her secret with a female student; thereby, she has role modeled for her student the importance of "doing your own thing, even if it makes you different."
- A female high school teacher learns karate; she then proceeds to drop kick about a dozen large thugs who harass her on the way to her car; thereby, she proves that women can be at least as tough on their students as men can be, especially men who haven't taken karate.
- Students in an economically/socially deprived city high school buckle down under the tutelage of a gifted teacher and proceed to pass their Advanced Placement (AP) tests in mathematics; thereby, they prove that with hard work, diligence, and a mammoth amount of sacrifice on the part of a single teacher, even underprivileged teenagers can succeed at the highest level.

Wait a minute! Stop the presses! That last storyline: Isn't it true? Didn't that actually happen?

Yup, Jaime Escalante, a Garfield High School (Los Angeles) Advanced Placement mathematics teacher, led fourteen of his formerly neglected students to passing the Big Kahuna of all tests, the AP exam, a test most serious students both covet, and dread, at the same time. Many viewers thought this movie to be a work of fiction, an impossible story about fourteen motley kids and an unlikely heroic teacher. But it wasn't fiction: it was mostly fact.

This success story supported three axioms about teaching:

1. Grand teachers can get grand results from any student.
2. Students who love and respect their teacher have a better chance of becoming successful in that teacher's class.
3. Hard work and sacrifice conquer all.

Because the story is true, and those kids did pass that exam, it is hard to deny empirical evidence. An exceptional teacher made extraordinary sacrifices and showed his students how to do the same. It is a good advertisement for the teaching profession; it puts teachers on a billboard and tells the world what is possible and can be achieved with time, effort, money, and hard work.

But do other teachers like that this happened?

Parents and the rest of society are the first to notice these kinds of phenomena. They pay close attention; they respond in kind. After telling the story of Jaime Escalante to several parents (most of them knew the story already or had seen the movie *Stand and Deliver*),[9] this author asked them to stand and deliver their opinions of the film: Why was it perceived as so extraordinary? What had they learned from it? What kinds of thoughts, feelings, and actions had the movie inspired in them?

From several responses, here are three (the disconcerting parts are in *italics*):

- It [*Stand and Deliver*] shows that if kids buckle down and concentrate on school, they can do better. They can always do better. *Sometimes all it takes is one good teacher to ignite a spark, to make a difference in their whole world.*
- I knew it! I knew that teacher could do it! *Mr. Escalante was far from lazy, like I'm afraid so many teachers are today.*
- Every teacher in America should be required to see this movie [if they hadn't already]. *There's a lot in there that every teacher could learn and apply to their own [sic] teaching careers.*[10]

Even if these comments aren't holding all teachers up to Jaime Escalante standards, they are clearly implying that teachers can do more—that teachers *should* do more in order to improve the quality of education their children are receiving.

So . . . when things go wrong, who is to blame? Unless a specific culprit can be identified, all that people have to do is look around and shrug, "I don't know whose fault this mess is. I really don't. But what I do know is that teachers could do more to fix it. Hey, have any of you guys seen *Stand and Deliver*?"

5. Are there accurate documentaries that describe the faultiness of America's teachers?

None that do so intentionally: in fact, quite the opposite is true. Sometimes a film—or a documentary—starts out attempting to elevate the status of teachers in society but winds up doing quite the opposite; at least, this is how a lot of people see it.

Stand and Deliver created an antagonistic environment for teachers. The public fell in love with Jaime Escalante; correspondingly, they fell in love with teachers. Even though the movie was not a documentary per se (Escalante was played by the gifted actor Edward James Olmos), for all intents and purposes, Olmos *was* Escalante. And although the public adored Olmos, they adored the character he played even more: *After all, look what one middle-age teacher can accomplish! If our teachers just put their minds to it . . . we need more men and women like Jaime Escalante in the teaching profession!*

Our teachers do put their minds to it . . . and their backs and hearts and souls—and, as will be seen later, their lives.

There's no hiding the incompetent teachers; there's no eluding that some teachers are downright lazy and avoid—at all costs—hard work. But that's not the totality of the problem for educators—far from it. The general public's perception—the political leaders' perception, too—that teachers can huddle together and be a panacea for all that it is wrong in America's schools daunts educators who know this is not true.

The mass media have created some delicious documentaries about teachers. Those on the inside, behind the cameras and in the splicing rooms, probably did not go out of their way to make life more difficult for America's teachers, but they wound up doing just that. The film documentary *Waiting for Superman* did not lack acclaim: the movie received the Audience Award for Best Documentary at the 2010 Sundance Film Festival.[11] It also won the "Best Documentary Feature" at the Critics Choice Movie Awards.[12]

The filmmakers figured they had a good one on their hands, but they weren't ready for the accolades that immediately came their way, from almost everyone.

In *Waiting for Superman*, Geoffrey Canada describes his journey as an educator and his corresponding surprise when he realizes, upon entering adulthood, that Superman is a fictional character. He concludes that no one is powerful enough to save everyone.[13]

Throughout the film, different aspects of American public education are examined. Concerns, such as the ease with which a public school teacher achieves tenure, the inability to fire a teacher who is tenured, and how the system fails to reprimand poorly performing teachers are shown to have an impact on the educational environment and, of course, a negative impact on all kids.

Teaching standards are called into question: the interpretations of those standards are often different at the school, state, or federal level. The corresponding confusion and leniency in interpreting standards is connected to drops in literacy and overall subject-matter competency.[14]

The film also scrutinizes teachers unions. Michelle Rhee, the former chancellor of the Washington, DC, public schools, attempts to take on the union agreements that teachers are bound to, but suffers a backlash from the unions and the teachers themselves. Teachers, in general—especially teachers unions and their leaders—are demonized in this movie, not just through the direct attacks they take (all anecdotal, with cameras placed in the right places at the right time, and interviews patently excised and edited) but by driving home the insinuation that all teachers need to be like the guy in the movie: the savior, the hero, the champion—Superman.

Everything must work in unity for the schools to work; but there is an abundance of frenzied accusation and finger pointing in the teachers' direction, including the notion that there aren't more charter schools because of teachers and their damn unions.[15]

In a perfect world, education would have its own Superman coming to save the day. (Or was that the slogan designated for Mighty Mouse?)[16] People would all be grateful to every teacher who works diligently with students—one-on-one, one to many, many to one—those who risk their lives, and some who lose their lives, because of their firm belief in a system that could work with their contributions. If only that system would not buckle under the strain of poverty and broken families and strained budgets and public apathy. If only. They would no longer be mortals—but Superman: every one of them.

Man, just where is Superman when the schools need him?

The movie detonated too many explosives and blew itself up. Four myths have been collected, and they are the premises for reading this book. These myths don't cover everything, not by a long shot; but they saddle society with the task of doing some serious thinking, before they call each other to arms against teachers, the lazy man's out when it has to do with education reform.

MYTH 1: In order to be saved, every kid needs a Superman.

Understanding that the premise of this film is to show that a belief in Superman is tenuous, at best, it is mind-boggling to watch Superman attempting to save, and succeeding at saving, children. University logic courses teach that anecdotal evidence is the worst kind unless coupled with data that actually mean something; yet, anecdotes rule this thin documentary. Giving *any* impression that deprived children need teachers over dedicated fathers, or community intervention over family guidance, should be seen as blasphemous.

Statistics scream of this depravity: boys who do not grow up in a home with their father are 75 percent more likely to wind up in prison, 80 percent more likely to live in poverty, and 110 percent more likely to drop out of school than boys who were raised by their fathers.[17]

Why is the clamor for Superman louder than the uproar about child abuse and permissive, neglectful child rearing? Maybe every kid needs a Superman, but not the kind they allude to in this documentary.

When Dave grew up, his father was as Superman-ish as it was going to get for him.[18] His father didn't own a gun and wouldn't have harmed even an invading spider, but he spent lots of time with Dave, talked with him, and, most important of all, he really loved him.

Dave, a black man who grew up in Long Beach, became a doctor. He never met the "Man of Steel." Not once. But he didn't need him: he had his dad.

MYTH 2: A dedicated teacher is the answer to the schools' woes.

Perhaps, thousands—maybe hundreds of thousands—of dedicated teachers are *an* answer, but just who is going to find them? Besides the fact that it is not the stated goal of American educators to bail children out of degenerate environments or to become Big Brother babysitters in lieu of derelict parents, the supposition that educators can provide a pea in every kid's pod runs faulty.

Waiting for Superman earns the ironic distinction of placing the blame on teachers while claiming to laud only certain teachers: a paradox of a dangerous magnitude. The film's contention that a teacher's intervention provides a universal remedy for salvaging a child's life, leads to this inevitable non sequitur: *Teachers today really suck! We don't have enough teachers like Superman! If only we did!*

MYTH 3: More than anything else in a child's education, a teacher matters.

Some would say that having a wonderful teacher is a child's catalyst for success. Having a strong teacher is extremely important to a kid's educational and vocational development, but it is not a panacea. Oodles of obsessions permeate children's lives, and the inner city child is no exception; indeed, distractions exist all around him: gangs, drugs, and various other criminal activities march to the forefront of concerns, in addition to the disruptions that cloud most other young people's lives: phones, video games, and parties. Teachers can do only so much about those.

But if I could only find that one teacher . . . !

This writer would never minimize the worth of a powerful teacher in a child's life. But Superman?

Outstanding, exceptional teachers are a fictional presence in *Blackboard Jungle, Dangerous Minds*, and—though they are not specifically mentioned—*Lucas Tanner, Welcome Back Kotter, Glee,* and other TV programs designed for the teenage palate. The fairly recent film *Spare Parts* reveres a dynamic *substitute* science teacher.[19]

In the real world, though, society has reasonable expectations of professionals. Citizens do not expect police officers to stop every crime or reverse the injuries of a murder victim. They don't assume firefighters will prevent every building in the city from burning to the ground and will resuscitate a child who expired from smoke inhalation.

It is irrational to expect America's teachers to perform comparably unreasonable tasks: saving children from the ravages of poverty and deprivation; opening the door to their souls so they may see the world from an altruistic, optimistic perspective; and erecting the personal infrastructure people require in order to exist happily, fruitfully, and sensibly in a challenging universe.

Other than Mom or Dad, no single individual should be *expected* to do those things: not one friend, one neighbor—or one teacher, someone who may have begun as a total stranger in the life of a troubled child.

MYTH 4: Waiting for Superman elevates our esteem for American teachers.

Nope.

Not even close.

A gullible public, backed by the jovial support of educators, have drunk the Kool-Aid: *Kids need miracle teachers; kids get miracle teachers. Teachers work miracles. If all kids had miracle teachers like these, they would thrive.*

Waiting for Superman injects an insidious sermon of contempt for most American teachers. Not the great teachers: the Superman teachers are exempt from scorn and ridicule; in fact, they are praised. The sparseness of these sensational teachers, however, propels the public, and politicians, to scratch their heads: *What's wrong with education? Why won't more teachers turn into those highlighted by Davis Guggenheim?*[20]

It's the unions.

Teachers' unions disdain tenure. Tenure protects even bad teachers. Bad teachers can't be fired. If bad teachers can't be fired, the kids don't learn. If kids don't learn, they can't get jobs. If they can't get jobs, their lives suck. See, not very complicated at all.

It's the bureaucracy.

Teachers could obliterate bureaucracy, but they don't. Perhaps, they don't choose to; perhaps, they choose to but are too lazy to carry out their intentions. Perhaps, the red tape, anonymous orders from afar, and administrative confusion from the near are too much for teachers to handle. And, again, the kids suffer for it. It's tough to excel under these mind-boggling conditions.

It's human nature.

Most people don't bother to excel at what they do. Most people, tolerant of mediocrity, are okay with barely getting by. With salaries that fall below trash haulers, teachers acquire little motivation to rise above the mediocre. They aren't staring at life-and-death situations every day; they are trying to figure out how to pay their mortgages. Driving to work in the morning and thinking about a scheduled meeting with a bankruptcy lawyer in the evening, can leak the air from the inspiration balloon.

It's the kids.

Everyone would agree that it's easier to be a competent teacher in a school where you are supported by parents and administrators. Rising to the level of distinction comes naturally if your community lends you respect and support, and if children are taught to revere teachers. Some kids, though, spend the night banging gangs, gang banging, or getting banged—whatever—and they walk into your classroom the next morning with groggy eyes and a smirk. Who wants to put up with that? Seriously. Superman would rather face kryptonite than a bunch of unruly, unkempt, prison-bound teenagers—or immature, neglected, drooling fourth graders, all of whom may be a real teacher's version of kryptonite.

It's the administrators.

Current fads and trends have taken the fun out of teaching. Teachers are creative people; they come up with interesting, sometimes unique, ideas. And they adapt these ideas to their individual personalities. Along comes the guy in the hopelessly out-of-date polyester suit, the guy who tells teachers in the district that the think tanks at the state capital have decided *what* they are going to teach, and *how* they are going to teach it, and *when* they are going to teach it: the amount of creativity garnished from such a setup can be measured in coffee spoons (to borrow a line from T. S. Eliot).[21]

Who wants to get up in the morning and slip into her robot suit for the rest of the day? Even windup dolls are more fun than robots: at least, windup dolls initially sport energy and enthusiasm before their windup thingy peters out. Teachers must be mavericks for them simply to survive under these conditions, let alone excel at their jobs and foster unprecedented accomplishments where they work.

The development of personal expectations is a healthy way of mapping roads to success. But teachers have enveloped themselves into a system of reward and punishment: if they measure up to what others envisioned, they are revered; if they fall short, they are mocked—or worse. Yeah, worse: they are *blamed* for all that goes wrong at home, work, and in society.

A typical conversation that takes place at the water cooler practically every day:

> *"I gotta go to the school and talk to my son's third grade teacher."*
> *"Yeah? Why?"*
> *"She's flunking him in math."*
> *"Math—really? Why?*
> *"He doesn't learn anything."*
> With a forced laugh: *"That's prob'ly because she don't teach him anything."*
> *"She doesn't."*
> *"Yeah, my son is in high school, and his teachers don't do much to help him, either."*
> *"Not like when we were kids . . . "*
> *"Yeah, the teachers today . . . "*
> *"They're lazy."*
> *"Lazy. Don't want to lift a finger—to do extra."*
> *"You got that right."*
> *"Lazy."*
> *"Right."*
> *"Did you see that* Waiting for Superman *movie?"*
> *"Yup. Came away wondering why all teachers can't be like that."*
> *"Me, too."*
> *"Teacher unions."*
> *"Yup."*
> *"And just plain lazy."*
> *"Yup. Lazy."*

Americans blame teachers for what is wrong with the schools. They are incapable, or unwilling, to understand the complexities, to look beyond the sensational headlines and talking heads' points they hear on FOX or CNN.

You can't fight a fire if you are putting water on the woodshed while the house is ablaze. Wishing it were the woodshed on fire, because a woodshed fire is easier to put out, won't save the house. America can't fix its schools by spanking its teachers because they don't live up to expectations spawned in schmaltzy movies and calculating documentaries.

Critiques of *Waiting for Superman* set the tone for repairing what ails America's educational institutions.[22]

Film critic Joe Williams of the *St. Louis Post-Dispatch* wrote, "[Director of *Waiting for Superman*] Guggenheim maintains that bad schools produce bad neighborhoods, rather than the other way around. He blames bad schools on bad teachers. And he blames bad teachers on bad unions. . . . Guggenheim doesn't reveal what percentage of teachers fall into that category [incompetent teachers]. Nor does he spend much time arguing that public-school teaching is hard work for relatively low pay in overcrowded classrooms full of kids whose discipline problems are exacerbated by their indifferent parents."[23]

And Steve Persall of the *Tampa Bay Times* observed, "Nobody can disagree that *Waiting for Superman* deals with a subject demanding attention. But it paints the engulfing problems of U.S. education with a brush too broad, and samples too small, to be definitive. Depending on any movie for all the answers would be an easy way out, and that's what got us here in the first place."[24]

These complex problems shouldn't be glossed over by turning to simplistic solutions. A subsequent examination of America's teachers entertains these complexities. It reveals secrets no one has heretofore released on a movie screen. The truth should be in the open for all to ponder. After all, the world of education is a distant cry from the fantasy of fiction.

NOTES

1. This film became the juvenile delinquent's mantra: suck in school, but an amazing, selfless, altruistic teacher will wind up saving the day.
2. Principal John Potts says he doesn't watch films like these. He gets too depressed when he thinks about what *really* swings through the doors of the faculty lounge.
3. The only people who can say this with a straight face are educators who are not in the classroom. People with a stake in upping the technology ante purport to know a lot about technology, but they really don't have a clue how it ties in with the fluidity of a well-run classroom. The truth is that it often doesn't. Sometimes setting the stuff up can take as much as thirty minutes. Other times, the technology refuses to work properly, or at all: precious time wasted.
4. Noah Glyn, "Jackson Toby on School Shootings," *National Review*, December 17, 2012, nationalreview.com/corner/335842/jackson-toby-school-shootings-noah-glyn.
5. Not his exact words, but the essence of how this teacher lived and what he believed is a teacher's role model.
6. Diana Lambert and Philip Reece, "New Teachers Scarce after State Funding Cuts," *Sacramento Bee,* March 7, 2014, Education Section, 1.
7. Barnett Berry (College of Education, University of South Carolina, Columbia), "Why Bright Students Won't Teach," *Urban Review* 18, no. 4 (1986): 276–79.
8. This FOX TV show (2009–2015) surprised the critics for six years on its way to winning every award imaginable. The teacher, Mr. Schuster, could be Superman. He's the closest thing to it; then again, it's just a show.
9. *Stand and Deliver*, directed by Ramon Menendez, Warner Bros., 1988.
10. These are beneficial comparisons and contrasts for the teaching *profession*, but detrimental comparisons and contrasts for the individual teacher.
11. Sundance takes place in Utah. It is the baby of actor/director Robert Redford.
12. The Broadcast Film Critics Association presents annual awards for both movies and television.

13. *Waiting for Superman*, directed by Davis Guggenheim, Paramount Vantage Entertainment, 2010.

14. Other than these little tidbits, this film is very pro-education.

15. *Waiting for Superman* does not place the blame squarely on the backs of teachers. To be fair, the movie makes strong indictments of teachers *unions*. However, the super teachers that emerge from the system the film attacks would still exist, with or without teacher tenure, school choice, or charter schools. As in other avenues of life, the cream has a way of rising to the top, the crap sinking to the bottom.

16. It was inspiring: Mighty Mouse would save the day. Little, squeaky voice—he would fix what was wrong, cure all ills, and do it inconspicuously. Teachers equipped with little, squeaky voices may find inspiration in Mighty Mouse.

17. FBI Crime Statistics, 1991: penetrating, breathtaking—but not at all surprising.

18. If Superman looked like a short, dumpy Mr. Clean, he would have looked like my father.

19. Guggenheim is the director of, and the mastermind behind, *Waiting for Superman.*

20. This interesting 2015 film, directed by Sean McNamara, told of students who were adept at building robots, an interesting premise, quite different from the notion of teachers *turning* students into robots.

21. The speaker in Eliot's poem, "The Love Song of J. Alfred Prufrock," talks about measuring his life in "coffee spoons," so this line may, or may not, have something to do with the point at hand. But it is a nice literary allusion, no?

22. These comments about the movie *Waiting for Superman* spawn the thesis of this text: one can't assume that a teacher (or a bunch of teachers) is going to save the system. The film's misleading direction is antithetical to its intent.

23. Joe Williams, "St. Louis Director Talks about *Waiting for Superman*," *St. Louis Post-Dispatch,* Oct. 8, 2010, Movies Section.

24. Steve Persall, "Education Documentary Gets Passing Marks," *Tampa Bay Times*, October 14, 2010.

Chapter Two

Frustration of Shame

Teachers,[1] a superb satire, cleverly portrays America's teachers in a light that makes teaching look like fun. A line uttered at the end of the film strikes a chord: Nick Nolte's high school history teacher character, Mr. Jurel, chidingly—with a flare of brutal honesty—says to his colleague, Ms. Hammond (JoBeth Williams), "Of course I'm crazy! I'm a teacher!"[2]

Why do regular, ordinary people become teachers? What possesses a seemingly normal man or woman to decide on teaching as a lifelong profession? Given the state of affairs, what on earth are those students in education schools thinking about—how did they ever convince their parents to support them in their decision to embark upon teaching as a career choice?

Most people simply dismiss these kinds of questions; apparently, they already have the answers.

But they don't. It's convenient for them to point to the spirit of Nick Nolte's line in the movie: *They're just crazy. They're teachers.* Logically, it follows suit: *Crazy equals teacher. Teacher equals crazy.*

Clinical diagnosis aside, most teachers are not officially crazy, just *apparently* crazy. Which is good enough for people to generalize about educators. Kindergarten teachers, and to some extent, elementary school teachers, are the craziest ones. They wipe the boogers from the faces of their students. They dodge sputum and vomit and manage to smile while doing it.

The worst thing a high school teacher is forced to wipe off the face of a student is an obnoxious smile, and he prides himself in his ability to do just that. Usually, a wry comment or a pointed sarcastic quip gets the job done. But none of this works with children who are not yet six or seven years old. High school teachers have special admiration for elementary school teachers. They also believe that these teachers are, in fact, nuts.

Before delving into the various reasons why people become teachers and *stay* in the profession, it's time to take a look at the biggest challenges for America's teachers. The truth about the challenges teachers face may be surprising. The general public doesn't focus on matters such as these; they mostly gloss over the complex issues and approach education concerns from the standpoint of their own experiences. These self-serving mechanisms make perfect sense; unfortunately, they detract from solving many of the problems in the education community and hamper the hiring and maintaining of excellent teachers.

Some teachers would find it easier to work in the coal mines.

1. Fatigue

What!?! You are comparing the effects of a teacher's workload to the fatigue of a coal miner's! You've got to be kidding!

Consider anecdotal support for the concept of teacher exhaustion:

The fatigue factor begins in the evening, before the next school day, compounding the lingering tiredness from previous days. It would be nice to begin each day of work fresh, well rested, but teachers quickly learn the only way to recharge their batteries is to sleep for a couple of centuries.

4:00 P.M.

An elementary school teacher returns home around four o'clock in the afternoon. Most elementary school teachers do not have a clue as to when they actually leave school. By that time, they are comatose.

7:00 P.M.

After washing dishes and putting away the dinner leftovers, the teacher begins to prepare for her fifth-grade classroom. Assuming her own children have quieted down, and this mother/teacher has managed to meet the demands of *her* kids, she can place herself in a reasonable position to get things ready for her workday tomorrow.

The elementary school teacher finds a well-lit corner of her living room to do her work. She prefers this to her bedroom or a private office. She wants to intermingle at least a little bit with her family. She finds it deserted, eerie in her seclusion. Yes, family can be distracting, but it is also the company that loves her.

7:30 P.M.

Finally: make up those flash index cards for math; complete a PowerPoint presentation on the Civil War; prepare notes for a discussion on *Sideways*

School; post grade scores on the school's website, even though most parents aren't intense about spelling quiz results for fifth graders.

9:30 P.M.

Watch a couple of Netflix reruns of *Breaking Bad*, a popular TV series about a high school chemistry teacher/drug kingpin who doesn't work nearly as hard or as many hours as this fifth-grade teacher. But he, nonetheless, ends up accumulating hundreds of millions of dollars. Very uplifting.

10:30 P.M.

Wind down the day with a warm bath, a hot shower, or a small dose of arsenic—whatever her mood suits her.

This is an *easy*, routine day, though it doesn't mention inevitable emergencies (parent contacts, faculty meetings, workshops, chew-outs by administrators, car crashes—intentional or accidental—on the way to work, clean-up of her classroom: the regular custodian has been restrained by illness, death, or budget cuts). During testing periods, it gets even more hectic; there is no rest for the weary.

5:30 A.M.

Get out of bed and take on the day all over again.

There may be children around, too. Her children. They require time, attention, and love. Most experts argue that her children should go to the top of her priorities pyramid.[3] And she could have a husband. She *should* have a husband. She *needs* a husband. But he requires attention, too, maybe even more than their kids do. A loving family can be fulfilling and wonderful. But it can also be exhausting. Many argue that there is no such thing as "a balance" between a work life and a private or home life. Those people are pragmatists: they contend you can't have it all. Pick something. When it comes to choosing between family and a profession, go ahead: select one.[4]

This discussion of teacher fatigue includes only that wearisome part of teaching that occurs outside the classroom, the extra burdens. But exhaustion inside the classroom is the primary culprit. Teaching is exhausting. Teaching is debilitating. Sure, it's possible to sit on your butt all day and pass out worksheets and dittos,[5] but that is not teaching. Most teachers aren't like that.

Perception is 90 percent of the process for judging teachers. And perceptions are wrong too often. They come from personal places that have absolutely nothing to do with fairness or objectivity.

The strains on K–12 classroom teachers are enormous. No, they don't rival the pressures on police officers, who stop ominous-looking people on street corners and in dark alleys; they don't compare with the stresses on firefighters, who rush into burning buildings close to collapse. But the constancy of stress and pressure and responsibility takes its toll on teachers. And teachers just wear down. They become exhausted, tired beyond description. Usually this erosion is insidious, hidden from them for a long time.

No, it's not the coal mines, but almost.

2. Compensation

Teachers make a decent salary. People say, "You ought to teach in California, Bertha. Teachers out there make good money."

In California. And whatever *decent* means—that is what teachers earn: a "decent" amount of money. But here's the deal about teachers' salaries in California: someone who lives in California is not salivating over the prospect of becoming a teacher and making around $60,000 a year. Maybe he is planning on driving a car to work every day. Has he seen the gas prices in California?[6] And try eating at a California restaurant. He has to take out a home equity loan to eat at the local dive. Owning a home would be a long shot. Buying property in California isn't cheap. Home prices have gone through the roof.[7]

How many teachers travel from their half-million-dollar homes in their new Mercedes to an upscale restaurant in New Rochelle? Okay, that was a ridiculous question, positioned on standards and expectations that have ridiculous connotations. So, let's put it this way: How many teachers travel from their $2,000-a-month apartment in their ten-year-old Honda to a McDonalds? Now we're talking! The number of teachers in this category is staggering.

Nobody goes into the teaching profession expecting to get rich. It is a cop-out of enormous proportions for teachers to complain about the meager amount of money they earn. They knew the situation. They studied in college and then in graduate school, fully understanding that they would never make as much money as a professional athlete or famous entertainer. So cut it with comparisons to LeBron James.

Considering all the work, commitment, sacrifice, and education that are expected from our teachers, their salaries lag big-time. But teachers rarely complain about this—at least, publicly. Most teachers gripe in private and let their boisterous unions officially do the talking for them.

In the monstrously popular television series *Breaking Bad*,[8] Walter White, a high school chemistry teacher, discovers he has terminal lung cancer. In order to make sure his wife and two children are financially secure after he dies—and, ultimately, for the purpose of paying the extravagant medical bills for his cancer treatment—White goes into the illegal-drug business with a former student of his. They manufacture and sell the highest quality methamphetamine that has ever existed.

Over six seasons, a lot happens on this show, but a question critics ask repeatedly is, "You mean, a teacher's salary and fringe benefits package don't pay for cancer treatment? How can that be?"[9]

Mr. White did have *some* medical coverage, just not enough to pay for everything. Billed for his deductible, he quickly sank into enormous debt. The show's writers concocted a plot that depended on New Mexico's teachers being shafted by their school boards.

In reality, educators in New Mexico are on one of the lowest teacher-pay scales in the United States.[10] Walter White's claims that he would wind up destitute by trying to pay his medical bills is not too far from the truth. Walter White ambles dolefully from the room where he is administered chemotherapy to the hospital's payments window, where he writes checks for thousands of dollars he cannot afford.

Viewers curse those lousy compensation packages that teachers earn! Teachers should be making at least enough money to pay for cancer treatment, for God's sake! Look at what is happening to Walter White: from being a docile, lovable teacher, he is turning into an egotistical, ruthless sociopath. Teachers should not have to face such cruel fates. Walter's medical insurance didn't pay for his cancer treatments. Thousands of dollars came from his pocket (from the streets) and into the hospital's coffers. This television series, which ran for six years and whose finale earned the highest ratings of any single cable television program in the history of the boob tube, did its part in promoting public empathy toward teachers—and drug dealers.

Compensation packages for teachers throughout America leave a lot to be desired. In some states (California, New York, and Massachusetts), teachers are given benefits packages fit for kings and queens. In other states (Mississippi, Alabama, Utah, Idaho), what teachers are offered in the way of medical insurance is embarrassing—not to mention, potentially devastating, to their lives and the well-being of their families.

Those who support teachers don't request these open-ended benefits, either. Not even close. But college-educated men and women who have attended professional graduate schools, men and women who spend an impressive 80 percent of their lives teaching, deserve more rewarding contracts. Most teachers admit they don't work for the money, but they must make money; they can't do it for free.

Any teacher who says he would do it for free is basing that declaration on the presumption that he won't make any money for teaching, but has a sustainable income from somewhere else. Either that, or he has a benevolent, charitable, and *extremely* understanding spouse.

3. Status

Who are lower on the professional totem pole than those who work primarily with children? Pediatricians are cast beneath cardiologists, child psychologists under adult psychologists. Teachers rank below lawyers (believe it or not), and high school teachers bear more professional status than do elementary school teachers. The younger the kids, the less society seems to think of the professions that are associated with children.

There are obvious exceptions. But it's true. Otherwise, teaching would be the most esteemed, sought-after profession in the United States—in the entire *world*. Men and women, fresh out of college, even the most prestigious universities on earth, would be flocking to join the teaching ranks. But they're not, because teachers care about prestige as much as a bagel maker cares about prestige. And for people who are hungry, *bagel maker* has more stature than does *teacher*.

This revolting development in the profession is a relatively new one. For generations, a teacher—albeit paid poorly by any measure of professional comparison—rang with an air of glory. Okay, *glory* might be stating it too strongly; *respectability* is more accurate.

When this author's father, then an eighth-grader, pushed his elocution teacher down a flight of stairs, the school not only kicked him out; they sentenced him to watch three consecutive weeks of women's professional basketball.[11] A hard—perhaps cruel and unusual—punishment, indeed. But if you treat your teachers with an agonizingly small amount of respect, your punishment should be equally agonizing.

A recent poll asked 100 college students at Cal State University, Fullerton, which jobs in the United States offered prestige. On a list of careers and professions, both public and private, *teacher* was ranked . . .

1. Doctor or surgeon
2. Military
3. FOX News TV analyst
4. Pharmacist
5. Engineer
6. Computers, programming
7. Law enforcement
8. Firefighter
9. Pornographer
10. Prosecutor

Hmm . . . ? Where is *teacher* on this list? Check it carefully. You'll see it. Won't you?

Teacher didn't make the top ten of the most highly respected professions/careers in America. Maybe it was number 11. The survey didn't indicate a number 11. Maybe the best—and most promising—thing that can be said about this poll is *professional athlete* didn't make the list, either.

However, compensatory factors exist that allay the feelings of a professional athlete: a baseball player makes more money in one year than a teacher will earn in fifty years.[12] That kind of thing makes up for the lack of prestige, although a guy who takes the field for the New York Yankees probably isn't suffering from a lack of self-esteem.

4. Degradation

That is a powerful word: *degradation*. It is a yucky word. If the shoe fits, the situation stinks. Here is a compilation of ten ways teachers across America feel degraded, simply for being hard-working schoolteachers. In no particular order:

1. Teachers are underpaid.
2. Administrators treat teachers like tall children.
3. The public thinks teachers are child molesters.[13]
4. Teachers must use their own money to buy supplies.
5. Kids and parents use social media to humiliate teachers.
6. Teachers ask permission to do the most basic of functions, such as taking a dump.[14]
7. College professors' salaries dwarf public school teachers' in comparative status.[15]
8. Teachers' public and private behaviors are scrutinized, analyzed, and often fictionalized.
9. Teachers often wind up as the central topic of conversation at Thanksgiving dinner.
10. Teachers are in a profession most parents (even those who are teachers) advise their children to avoid.

Let's look separately at each of these areas of degradation.

Ah, on second thought, no need to do that: each of them speaks for itself.

5. Humiliation

Mrs. Trask forgot everything at home. She almost forgot her head, but it was attached to her body. She left behind her trusted folder, which included the material she needed in order to teach her eighth-grade American history class. She was fatigued from her preparation for Back to School Night; she didn't realize she had no folder until her students began to file into her classroom. She calmly—albeit, tiredly—opened her briefcase, and, much to Mrs. Trask's horror, her folder, usually in plain view, wasn't there.

The bell rang. Class was supposed to begin.

And Mrs. Trask suddenly realized she had to wing it.

She was not good at "winging it." Reality overcame her sense of equilibrium, for Mrs. Trask knew that humiliation lay right around the corner.

Thirty-two seventh-grade boys and girls in front of her chatted loudly, their way of waiting for her to begin class. But their teacher had no materials. She would improvise with workbooks and other resources she had stocked in her classroom, but she had become upset by her forgetfulness and lack of coherent organization. That alone thwarted her ability to succeed.

She reminded herself that she should be punished for being such a twit.

Although she was smart enough—and logical enough—to see the error in that kind of thinking, she badgered herself for making a difficult life of a junior high school teacher even more difficult.

And, so, here are the ten predominant sources of humiliation for America's teachers:

1. Embarrassments caused by forgetfulness or other mental lapses [16]
2. Others' social media postings
3. Lapses in judgment, leading to a lack of verbal professionalism [17]
4. Lambastes by administrators in front of students or other faculty member
5. Visible inability to pass rigorous exams and tests for professional promotions
6. Verbal assaults by parents [18]
7. A reversal of the presumption of innocence
8. Others becoming privy to personal information about low salaries and compensation
9. Compulsions to compare or contrast intelligence with colleagues or students
10. Failing to know an answer to a problem or a special question from a student, another teacher, or an administrator

Sometimes being a teacher can be downright embarrassing. It also can be uncomfortable simply *admitting* to being a teacher. When others ask their profession, teachers often mumble their answers under their breath or pretend they are sneezing when they reply with *teacher*.

By way of summary about teachers' plight on humiliation: teachers are supposed to be dignified. This means behaving in a dignified manner. Exactly what dignity means may differ from person to person. But it clearly is not dignified for a teacher to get into a verbal jousting match with parents, mix with students and colleagues in competitions of wit and intelligence, or turn twenty-five shades of red when coming to terms with not knowing the answer to a student's question:

"Mr. Rivera?"

"Yes . . . ?"

"In *To Kill a Mockingbird*, how did Scout and Jem's mother die?"

Mr. Rivera pauses; his face turns ashen. He then musters a boastful tone that is pure theater. He says, "She was run over by a car."

Which is not true.[19]

Nothing can be done here in order to save Mr. Rivera from humiliation. In retrospect, he should have known the answer to the question. He could have reversed his fate by asking the student what *she* thought about how Scout's mother had died. Or he could have opened the question up for discussion, hoping at least one student knew the answer. He would have projected more authority, and less mortification.

If this sort of occurrence is common, Mr. Rivera has a problem. But occasional embarrassment is part of the game. It goes with the territory. As with any occupation, those in education screw up every once in a while. All this usually means is shaking one's head, taking a deep breath, and going forward. Others customarily forget the occasional hiccup; life goes on.

Imagine being the smartest one in the room, or the individual *thought* to be the smartest—and clearly the oldest—one in the room, and finding out you are not the smartest one in the room. Or even the wisest, which is where, despite your seniority, you have let everyone else down in both departments. You are on display. *Here is Mrs. Franco! She is the smartest person here—and the oldest and wisest!*

But Mrs. Franco blew two answers on the key to the math quiz. And, later, when a rude and insensitive (soon to be suspended) student told her she was stupid, she began to shake and stutter like no one had ever seen her shake and stutter before.

The suicide rate among teachers is higher than you might think (or lower, depending on your image of teachers). *Teacher Mental Health* reported a few years ago: "The figures fluctuate, and it is hard to judge how much significance should be attached to the increase [in teacher suicides] from 2001 to 2010 (86%). However, the figures do suggest a general upward trend in teacher suicides over the 9-year period."[20]

Pressure abounds. Lily Duster, teacher/writer, observed, "In case you haven't noticed, we are the evil enemy, demonized as the most poignant problem that faces education today. On the radio in the morning on my way to work: Mayor Bloomberg is at war with NYCs [sic] teachers."[21]

Teachers have failed to meet public expectations. Whatever those expectations, stress comes from all around, every corner of society. The pressure cooker boils over, and sometimes teachers explode in anguish or anger or angst . . . or all three. A teacher's unique position places her in the position of being a god to children and parents.

But God isn't supposed to turn red in the face.

6. Hopelessness

Having access to upward mobility matters. Stagnant jobs attract the incompetent and the desperate. Most professions offer workers a chance to promote themselves; thus, they make more money and accumulate offers for better jobs, with even greater opportunities. The system perpetuates itself. But the motivation for men and women to work hard and make great sacrifices is apparent: eventually they win: they do make more money. They do advance up the ladder in their chosen careers. And they do land positions that broadcast prestige and esteem.

Potter Sturgeon, a veteran teacher of twenty-two years in the public schools system, retired in 2012. When asked to reflect upon his career, he was asked what his biggest regret was. "Stagnation," he responded determinedly. "At first, when I had been wide-eyed and youthful, I saw my career in education as a system of steppingstones—steppingstones to the prize at the end."

The prize was not necessarily one of monetary advancement; it wasn't one of reigning power. Mr. Sturgeon saw his rewards accumulated in the form of successes with his students: those who passed his classes who may not have passed without his help; those who came back to the school and told Mr. Sturgeon how much he had meant to them; those who went on to become professional or creative successes themselves; those whose very lives he may have saved, simply because they had listened to Mr. Sturgeon's advice; those who later won awards and honors, including service in the military; those who contributed to their communities; and those who went on to fulfilling political careers.

You may want to scratch that last one.

Teachers want to change the world. Ask practically any young person who is struggling in college: he will tell you he hopes to make money. That's why he is going to college. College graduates earn more money, receive more admiration, and gain more status. Isn't that still the perception? Are things different today? The state of the world, the condition of the economy, and a shift in values have made an impact on college students, once wide-eyed and bushy tailed, who are now pessimistic and cynical.

Even so, those who have opted to go into education, to become mentors of young people, have carted off a different set of goals and ambitions that have accompanied their journey into the adult world: money has not been *the* object, but merely *an* object. For budding young teachers, their clearly voiced desires have centered around being able to change the world; to make hurting young people whole; to take a system mired in indifference and make it into a system glowing with optimism about the future.

Unfortunately, the end product has come out with glitches and flaws. Sometimes the product hasn't come out at all because it never reached the point in which it could be of value.

In parts of the country, high school dropout rates have come down.[22] But in various places in America, students do not reach high school. Worse: some parents refuse to send their children to school at all, or they are apathetic about their kids' refusal to attend school.

Home schooling is on the rise, and that ain't good.[23] While the debate about the value—or ultimate success—of home schooling rages, one thing is certain: there are positives and negatives. For the children who were let down by their parents' home-school experiment, their personal failure is not about numbers and percentages. They received the short end of the stick. They would have been far better off in a *school* that worked.

The question ultimately becomes . . . *who let the students down?*

This book is about exposing the truth about those who are responsible for the failure of our schools—or, at least, who are *most* responsible. When teachers are blamed, especially when they are designated the primary culprits in perpetuating a system that is abominably ineffective, teachers suffer. They feel maligned. They lose their focus. They get sick.

They quit.

Sometimes they die.

Their feelings of hopelessness accent their frustration with the career they dreamed about all their lives, and finally achieved. This hopelessness leads to a shame beyond their control, out of their sphere of influence. It is a frustration of shame, compounded by despair: a sense that no matter what they say or do, nothing is going to change; ultimately, teachers will be blamed, ridiculed, and maligned for problems that have exploded into the public's eye.

A frustration of shame among America's teachers has become epidemic. The tragedy is that the real problems will stay unsolved, and the true culprits in the system will remain free to continue along their paths to destroy America's schools. The victims, America's children, won't even know what hit them.

NOTES

1. *Teachers*, directed by Arthur Hiller, United Artists, 1984: a teacher movie a cut above most others. Too bad hardly anyone saw it.

2. Ditto. Or was that Mr. Ditto? You have to see this fine film to get the "in" joke here.

3. Duh! Like it takes an expert to figure this one out! Yet, despite what we know to be true, it's often easier said than done, more easily preached than practiced. . . . You can lead a horse to water, but . . . never mind.

4. Sounds harsh. It's an objective truth. Pick one. A teacher friend said that when he first became a teacher, he was a perennial, perpetual nag. He nagged his students all day at school; he continued nagging when he got home, where it was his teenage daughters he nagged. He looked worse for the wear. Having two teenage daughters is akin to having been a first responder at ground zero in Hiroshima. Did you ever see how bad some of those people looked? Even today's teachers look better than first responders after a nuclear attack. But parents of teenage daughters look worse than all of these.

5. The ditto machine used to be the central focus of teachers in the faculty lounge. An ancestor of the Xerox machine, the ditto machine made copies of documents according to how fast you turned the crank on the machine. The copies were purple. And wet. But they smelled really good, a teacher's equivalent of glue sniffing.

6. As of this writing, gas prices are down. Prices could be hovering around five bucks a gallon by now.

7. In early 2016, home prices went through the roof. Homes in neighborhoods with schools that have a bad reputation—they went through the floor.

8. *Breaking Bad*, AMC, 2008–2014: Teachers loved this show. Every teacher who regularly watched thought it was about him.

9. A teacher's benefit package will pay for cancer treatment. As with anything else, there are differences in the quality of medical benefits; however, if you are a teacher with cancer, your benefits should take care of you, at least, to the point in which your finances are manageable. If you should happen to croak, it won't be because you were jilted in the medical insurance department.

10. Hailey Heinz, "What Do APs Earn?" *Albuquerque Journal*, March 1, 2012, 1.

11. This has nothing to do with education. It was merely a weak attempt to be funny. This attempt is hereby withdrawn. Forget about it. Very tasteless and inappropriate.

12. Figures are based upon a projected average salary for teachers and a low-end salary for a ballplayer, who makes around 87 trillion bucks a year.

13. See Salem witch hunts.

14. See chapter 10, which discusses this most basic of a teacher's bodily functions.

15. College teachers ($86,000) make more money than public school teachers ($72,500) near the top of the pay scale. That's an average salary.

16. Also known as spending too much time with your smartphone.

17. Too many lapses in judgment and one should not be teaching. Bad judgment is high on the list of justifications for teacher dismissal.

18. Actually, their responses could have been entertained, but they probably would have been fired. In 2001, in Kansas, a father lay in wait for his son's ninth-grade math teacher to leave his home for school. The father ran the teacher over with his car. Although he did not kill the teacher, he sent a strong message: teach better . . . or else!

19. How *did* their mother die? It's a good thing that she died, though; otherwise, one of the greatest novels ever would not have worked nearly as well.

20. "Teacher Suicide Rates." *Teacher Mental Health*, July 15, 2011, http://teachermentalhealth.org.uk/teachersuicide.html.

21. Lily Duster, "Teachers Committing Suicide: When Will the Bashing Stop?" January 14, 2012,http://americasfutureinsidestory.blogspot.com/2012/01/teachers-committing-suicide-when-will.html.

22. Emma Brown, "The Nation's High School Dropout Rate Has Fallen," November 15, 2015, *Washington Post*, Education Section, 1.

23. Jennifer Miller, "Increasing Number of Homeschooled Kids Suggests Need for Education Reform," December 16, 2015, https://www.noodle.com/articles/k12-homeschooling-on-the-rise184.

Chapter Three

It Ain't the Coal Mines

In the 1999 movie *October Sky*, the filmmakers take some great liberties describing the plights of coal miners in Tennessee. To watch this film, you would think coal miners in the 1950s and 1960s had it tough.[1]

Jack Saxton, a high school science teacher, watches *October Sky* with his students at the beginning of every school term. When he was about ten years old, he saw another film, one that now reminds him of *October Sky*. Jack had watched *Matewan* with his father. The movie was about the difficulties faced by coal miners in West Virginia. When he says "difficulties," he is referring to men who got up at three o'clock in the morning and jaunted over to the local coal mine, where, on a daily basis, they risked explosions, cave-ins, and black lung disease.

This notion of hard work and danger seemed rather odd to Jack, not to mention *ridiculous*. But he was only ten: What did he know about going to work and having to pay bills?

He remembers asking his dad, "Why do these men get up and go to work in those mines? Are they crazy?"

His dad, his usual stoic self, shrugged. "Because they have to."

"Why do they have to?"

"Because they buy food for their families."

It took a while for Jack to admire the coal miners: at first, he scoffed at them. He listened to what one of his teachers had said about coal miners having no education, no marketable skills, and no passions or hobbies. He'd figured these guys were stuck in the mines because they were underachievers, anonymous cogs in his country's economic machine.

Some of that was true: they were cogs in the economic machine. But they were very important cogs. Without miners, the gross national product of the United States would have gone down billions of dollars, maybe more. U.S.

efforts during the world wars would have been compromised, perhaps to a disastrous level of vulnerability.[2] Without miners to kick around and undermine, what would Democrats have to do during political campaigns? The miners mattered; they mattered a lot. And *somebody* had to do that mining.

It would be smart to look at the aforementioned missing qualities for which the coal miners were criticized. What are they? How important are they? And how in the heck do coal miners have anything to do with defending America's teachers?

No Education: At the risk of sounding like lyrics from a Pink Floyd song,[3] those coal miners "didn't have no education." What they *did* have was a powerful commitment to their wives and children: to put in a full day's work for a full day's pay; to uphold their dignity by doing a job that was both respectable and legal. Melbourne Johnson wrote, "His [a coal miner's] job was never finished. The frightening hours in the mines were followed by the daunting task of having to get enough rest and sleep, of having to eat well in order to maintain one's health and energy levels, and spending time with family."[4]

Coal miners did not go to college and study from dusty old books. Their task was to *perform*, not to study performing. Their role was to *produce*, not to learn the theories of production; they came to their careers with heart. The result of their toils was safer families and a better nation. Meeting the challenges of being a coal miner meant that everybody won: society, families, and coal miners.

When sympathizers shake their heads and wag their fingers about how difficult the miners' lives were, how despicable the conditions in which they worked, how overwhelming their challenges, it would behoove them to understand one basic concept: nobody told the miners it was going to be easy; nobody lied to them.

No Marketable Skills: Have you seen one of those late-night infomercials in which they talk about "having marketable skills"? *Sign up for our promotional deal. Learn how to market yourself. Learn skills you can market while you're learning how to market yourself; in fact, market yourself while you're learning about marketing yourself.* Whatever.

Ten years ago, a study by some of the largest Fortune 500 companies indicated the top skills they were seeking during the hiring process: (1) ability to communicate orally, (2) ability to express oneself through written discourse, and (3) ability to compute and work with numbers.[5]

Much has changed since then.[6]

Back in the old days, marketable skills had other meanings, other connotations. A young man about to graduate from high school considered his future in a different light. He wasn't thinking about computers and cell phones and video games. Because he was thinking about *surviving*, his requisites included attaining subsistence-level living. A good résumé today might be padded with experiences in technology and degrees in medicine; *back then* a good résumé indicated a willingness to work hard, commit to the company, and take risks. That made a person marketable.

In bygone days, "marketable" had more to do with character than with creativity—or even productivity. A tough, rugged dude would show up at the plant to apply for a job. But if he didn't pass the screening process, which often meant a series of verbal questions and a quick size-up by the bosses, he wouldn't get through the front door.

No Passions or Hobbies: The coal miners of Pennsylvania had passions and hobbies. Those passions and hobbies were different from today's passions and hobbies. In fact, by the standards *then*, the passions and hobbies of today might be irrelevant:

So, Don, what do you do in your spare time?
Go on my computer.
To do what?
Well, that's kind of personal, but I spend a lot of time on the Internet.
How will that help you be a better miner?
Silence.

Coal miners may have done a lot of manual work before they landed a job in the mines: pipe fitting, foundation laying, drywall coating, metal sheeting—the possibilities were endless. Unlike today, men would go right from high school into jobs that afforded them an opportunity to buy a home, get married, and provide for a wife and children. There were no credit cards, no home equity loans, no federal-state welfare programs. Families would help each other out, but financial limitations usually didn't permit much support. Hobbies and outside interests were what made certain men marketable and other men not as marketable.

Men, and sometimes women, took jobs they didn't necessarily want—that were outside the purview of their "dream jobs"—because they *had* to. Sure, society turned out a number of college graduates, the would-be doctors and lawyers and accountants—and teachers—but those who eventually became coal miners did so because they had special skills. It didn't make them better workers or nicer people; it made them coal miners.

Around the time that Jack's father was pointing out the hazards, and virtues, of working every day in the coal mines, Jack was beginning to wonder in what direction his own life was headed. Frankly, coal mining looked pretty darn good to him: a constant paycheck, enough money to support a family, a job title that (let's face it) stoked the women a little bit. (He later learned that the only hardhats that turned on women sat on the heads of firemen.)

Jack possessed none of the marketable skills to become a coal miner; he would have made a terrible coal miner. He hated dirt. He hated soot. He hated black lung disease. Everybody hated black lung disease, but he *really* hated it. And he was claustrophobic. Even elevators make him nauseous.

If Jack's whole family moved to West Virginia so he could pursue his dream of working in the coal mines, he never would have made it through the job-screening process; plus, he would have shown up for the coal miner job interview in a white shirt and a tie: not exactly a lure for the future bosses of a nice Jewish boy from California who sought employment refuge nearly a quarter of a mile under the earth's surface.

Jack had no marketable skills—at least, for coal mining.

What he *did* know how to do was talk. He found he liked teaching other people, allowing them to discover what he knew.

This was definitely preferable to being lowered into the ground on a gurney. The coal mines had lost their luster. He wanted his own classroom, not his own carbide lamp.

Jack has thought about those contrasts between what he'd once thought was an attractive way to spend his life (picking away in the mines), and what he had become (picking away at a child's defense mechanisms). And he was glad he became a teacher. He could have chosen coal mining, or any other profession in which he actually had to work for a living.

Here are five discernible differences between a career as a coal miner and a career as a schoolteacher. Notice how the arguments in favor of teaching over coal mining are a clever metaphorical defense—not necessarily of teaching itself—of America's teachers, in general. Perhaps, *clever* is not s strong enough word to describe these career comparisons!

1. Coal miners are paid by the hour; teachers are not.

It varies by state: coal miners in the United States are paid forty to sixty dollars an hour. Administrative positions, not the guys who go into the mines and do the actual work, are paid quite a bit more; some of them are salaried.[7]

Full-time classroom teachers are normally paid salaries, the depth and breadth of which depend on the states in which they work—and on the particular school district that hires them. These salaries can be anywhere from $35,000 a year (Mississippi), to $110,000 a year (Illinois). Teachers in New York and Connecticut are slightly behind Illinois.[8] Teachers in Canada make more money than those in the United States.[9]

While it may be fashionable for teachers and their unions to complain about how little they are paid, sometimes the truth does not support their claims. Sure, if one compares teachers' salaries to those of doctors or lawyers in private practice, teachers come out on the short end of the stick.[10] Doctors and lawyers, however, aren't blown to smithereens when something goes wrong—a loose screw in their office swivel chair—in the environment in which they work.

And doctors and lawyers don't wind up with black lung disease.

Johnson Craft, a popular high school teacher in California,[11] was succinct: "I would like to make more money. . . . When you talk about the comparative worth to society of a NBA player and a full-time science teacher who works in the inner city with disadvantaged kids, a teacher's value is so much greater. But who am I to complain? I chose my profession. I knew what I would get paid, and I had an idea how tough the job would be. . . . The money isn't that bad."

And it ain't the coal mines, Mr. Craft.

Coal miners would love to get their summers off, their working environments cleaned up, and their jobs protected by something comparable to teacher tenure. They don't have those luxuries. They work for less money; their job protections are minimal. And their lives are perennially at risk.

2. Coal miners are vulnerable to losing their lives; teachers are relatively safe.

The National Association for Coal Miner Safety and Recall reported last year, "Twenty-two deaths occurred on the job in the nation's coal mines. . . . Over the past ten years, 122 miners have lost their lives on the job."[12]

These statistics do not take into account (1) long-term deaths because of lung disease or other illnesses that can be traced to the mines; (2) heart attacks, strokes, or other sudden death episodes that may be related to the mines; or (3) homicides brought upon miners' families and friends because of the stress of working a mile under the earth ten hours a day, with impending death and injury hovering.

Contrasts with a miner's life fifty to one hundred years ago would be unfair because conditions today are so different (thanks to the unions that managed to push laws and policies to protect the lives of coal miners). However, death still lurks, and the suspense of working under these types of conditions takes its toll mentally and emotionally.

The United States Survey Course on the Web dramatically describes life in the coal mines for a young man who works there in order to help provide for his mother and sisters. His father was killed in the mines several years before.

> Outside the sun shone brightly, the air was pellucid [clear], and the birds sang in chorus with the trees and the rivers. Within the breaker there was blackness, clouds of deadly dust enfolded everything. . . . I tried to pick out the pieces of slate from the hurrying stream of coal, often missing them; my hands were bruised and cut in a few minutes; I was covered from head to foot with coal dust, and for many hours afterwards I was expectorating some of the small particles of anthracite I had swallowed.[13]

Wait, America's teachers: it gets worse.

The same young man:

> The coal is hard, and accidents to the hands, such as cut, broken, or crushed fingers, are common among the boys. Sometimes there is a worse accident: a terrified shriek is heard, and a boy is mangled and torn in the machinery, or disappears in the chute to be picked out later smothered and dead. Clouds of dust fill the breakers and are inhaled by the boys, laying the foundations for asthma and miners' consumption.[14]

As we all know by now, these horrendous working conditions have been described on numerous occasions in film, but they have also been put into lyrics. "Working in a Coal Mine," written by Allen Toussaint, does justice to the miners' plight.

> Five o'clock in the mornin,' I'm already up and gone
> Lord, I'm so tired, how long can this go on
> 'Cause I make a little money, hauling coal by the ton
> But when Saturday rolls around, I'm too tired for having fun
> Well, I'm working in the coal mine, going down, down, down
> Working in the coal mine, whoop, about to slip down
> Working in the coal mine, going down, down, down
> Working in the coal mine, whoop, about to slip down[15]

When it comes to their health and safety, teachers are in a different situation. The National Safety Council's Report on Public Employees reported, "In 2014, there were 135 teachers who died while on the job."[16] Presumably, they were at their schools when they took their last gasps. Without trying to minimize anyone's death, 135 teachers is a surprisingly small number relative to the four million teachers who went to work on a daily basis in 2014. A few more heart attacks and strokes among teachers would not have been surprising. Sixty-eight of those teachers committed suicide.[17] Some of them took their lives on the grounds where they taught school![18]

Teachers die younger than doctors do, but they live longer than those in most blue collar jobs, people who actually have to work for a living.[19] Although the life expectancy for teachers is higher than for that of career coal miners, the average survival rate for teachers is a little more than *two years* after the initial date of their retirement, which is the shortest retirement survival rate of any public-employee profession.[20]

Offhand summaries:

1. Teachers kill themselves; coal miners *get* killed.
2. Teachers are less likely to die on the job than coal miners.
3. Teachers don't have a heck of a lot of time left after they retire.
4. More teachers are murdered than are coal miners. (A teacher will live longer than a coal miner if she is not murdered.)

5. The workplace can be potentially hazardous for teachers—come on!—but not as hazardous as it is for coal miners.

Give or take a few unscheduled deaths or violent attacks in places of employment for coal miners and teachers, coal miners are clearly at a disadvantage when it comes to health and safety issues.

3. Coal miners are afforded no creative outlet on the job; teachers may be as creative as they want to be on the job.

If a coal miner tries to be creative, he may kill someone. There are only so many ways to detonate explosives so they do not blow up the whole coal mine and everything in it. Any job in which workers are conditioned by rote movements becomes excruciatingly boring after about ten minutes, let alone ten or twenty consecutive years. The monotony can be distracting, leading to a hazardous movement or an unproductive afternoon.

Teachers, on the other hand, have more latitude in their choices than do coal miners. A survey of elementary school teachers in Michigan reveals that the number one reason college graduates selected *elementary school teacher* as their profession was that that level of teaching allowed them more freedom to be creative. They thought (at least, initially) working with younger children would allow them more options in teaching modalities.

More inevitable truths, however, about teacher creativity:

1. Elementary school teachers are scrutinized more than other teachers. Level administrators keep in touch with school administrators about teacher job performance. Parents watch them like hawks. And they should; after all, we are talking about little children here. Can a teacher still be creative while others are carefully watching her and judging her? Yes. And no.
2. Newer curriculum guidelines, through programs like Common Core, have pulled in the reins on teacher creativity. Individual teachers may decide between using a marshmallow or a plum to conduct the science experiment, but they still must do that science experiment at about the same time other teachers who teach their grade level are conducting experiments with marshmallows and plums.
3. Teachers who use creative teaching methods in their classrooms are more apt to get fired for mysterious or unusual reasons, charges that tenure can't protect against. These folks may fall into the creepy or weirdness category, which may have come from their reputations for creativity, and the end result is termination.
4. Teachers tend to be creative because they are bored and require new and interesting ways to spend their time with students, who, by the

way, just happen to be *children*. "Creative" often connotes *experimental*, and it takes little unorthodoxy before there are public outcries about experimenting with our children.[21] Most teachers have thought a few kids they taught *should* have been experimented *on*, just to find out from which species they may have evolved.

5. Creativity may be an innate part of a teacher's personality. Some teachers know exactly how to get the kids interested in the subject matter. It isn't a trick, either. They don't lie or promise or bribe. They simply figure out how to make themselves likable to children and get their students to trust them. What separates this trait from the modus operandi of a coal miner is that the personality of the coal miner has zilch to do with effectiveness in mining; whereas, the personality of a teacher has *everything* to do with effectiveness as a teacher. In other words, improving a personality—perhaps, a temporary acting job—conducive to good teaching and communication may have a direct correlation to the level of a teacher's productivity and the way his students view him.

Teachers create their own persona. Many do it naturally. They are gifted from the get-go with a personality suited to the stage on Broadway or a comedy club in the heart of the Sunset Strip; others detect an urgency for them to do *something*: they do it through personality changes or voice changes or physical changes. But they do it. And that allows for a greater connectedness with students. The students learn more from these teachers, and that's what matters.[22]

4. Job growth in coal mining is unlikely; job growth in teaching is inevitable.

First, consider the difference in life expectancies; second, consider that when someone is dead, there is not a lot of room for his job growth.

Most people face periods in their lives when they feel as though they are stuck: in their home lives, in their personal lives, in their professional lives. The majority, however, move on. They graduate from their homes and families; they settle the differences and fix the rumblings in their personal lives. But when stuck in a career that gives them grief, they have but a few choices: they can quit their job, do something to get fired, or make changes in the place they have decided to remain.

Even as some moan and groan, they remain static, although the moaning and groaning gets louder and more pathetic as time passes. But that's all that changes: the intensity of the complaining. Teachers have it bad? Consider the opportunities for job advancement in the coal mining industry.

The National Association of Coal Miners released the following information—as gathered by the various unions that represent the rank and file:

"There are but a few ways that the harried drone gets to rise to the thrones of the royal princes. And they are almost impossible to achieve. . . . One may get an appointment based on competency, seniority, or that unfettered contingency called nepotism. . . . None of that is pleasurable . . . all of it is bias . . . and very little of it ever happens anyway."[23]

Most administrators in the upper echelon of the coal mining industry have not rushed into the top tiers from the ground level. They are almost always anointed from the beginning.

In education, teachers may strive to become administrators, but coal miners who pick away underground do not advance from point A to point B. Typically, they enter at point A, and they stay at point A. If they are among the fortunate, they will stay at point A for the duration. That duration will be measured in terms of decades, not in years or months. To be removed from point A is to be removed permanently: these men are dead.

Teachers don't work in the coal mines. Even when they enter at the very bottom of the totem pole (or whatever the hierarchy of teacher employment is called), they have a chance to move up the ladder—um, the pole. In almost every school district in the nation, a teacher's seniority (and salary) is based on how long she has remained employed in a particular school district. The longer she stays, the more seniority she has—and the more money she makes.

Teachers may go back to college and enhance their earning potential. For example, the 2015 salary schedule for a moderately sized school district in Southern California pays from $51,635 to $98,456 for a ten-month school year.[24] The lower end applies to a teacher with a bachelor's degree in her first year of service. The higher end is for a teacher with a minimum of thirty years in that same district, with a master's degree, and an additional forty-five upper-division credits.

She may earn more money by taking additional college courses. Alternatively, she may add to her seniority and earn more money, even if she never goes back to school at all, as long as she continues to accumulate years to her employment experience for the same school district.[25]

There are, of course, teachers who want to become administrators. Why a teacher would want to become a principal, assistant principal, or district paper pusher is hard to figure out. But putting the title of *principal* or *assistant superintendent* near a name delivers that sensation of power to a certain kind of person. George Bernard Shaw said, "[Power] means responsibility; that is why so many men dread it."[26]

Obviously, those who have advanced to a position of administrator did not dread they would one day finally arrive at that position. To the contrary, they worked hard, paid a lot of money, and ignored (at least, for a while) their loved ones. It takes time and effort to become an administrator; ultimately, administrators take the rap for much that goes wrong with our schools. (They don't always take the rap; teachers often catch undeserved hell.) Administrators are on the lines begetting ideas and laws, and pushing out orders and proclamations.

It's tough being an administrator. But it is a promotion, a few steps up the professional ladder from teacher. And for that, administrators are paid well. A high school principal in the formerly referenced school district in California makes $140,000 a year and receives a Cadillac medical program. For that, add another annual $20,000 that the district pays.[27]

A schoolteacher who wants to elevate his job description to *school administrator* must do the following:

1. secure a master's degree in education
2. obtain special credentials (regular teaching credentials don't suffice)
3. train on the job for one semester (affiliated with, and paid to, a university program)
4. arrange for an MRI in order to determine what has gone wrong with his brain

If, and when, a teacher is hired for an administrative position, she assumes a job that is not protected by tenure or by any other form of due process. In most states, she will not lose tenure in a particular school district *as a teacher*, but once she is forcibly removed from an administrative position, she is returned to a classroom assignment, often under the most dastardly of conditions.[28] If the canned administrator never *taught* in the district—or taught fewer than two or three years—she has no tenure and winds up pushing a stolen shopping cart on the street.

If you happen to be a teacher, you should not revel in promises of job promotion. True, in contrast to a coal miner, you may grow by leaps and bounds in your possibilities for professional advancement; however, a realistic understanding of what ordinarily happens to promoted teachers is important for making wise decisions about your career path.

This understanding may not be good for your sobriety: during their careers, only 7 percent of teachers meet the qualifications for becoming school administrators—on *any* level. Of that measly 7 percent, two-thirds obtain a position in administration. Of that approximately 3–4 percent—ready for this?—slightly more than half voluntarily leave their posts before they are ready to retire from education. Which means a minuscule percentage of teachers advance to, and remain in, their so-called job advancement positions.[29]

But congratulations for temporarily receiving a job promotion: better than coal miners usually get.

5. Coal miners do not have advocates; teachers have advocates.

Coal miners belong to unions. South Carolina is a right-to-work state; they don't have unions there. Pennsylvania and West Virginia have coal miners unions, but they don't do much to protect miners. Since the early part of the twentieth century when they made about five cents an hour and came up gagging and choking from the mines at six o'clock every evening, coal miners have made tremendous strides in salaries, benefits, and working conditions. These gains have been due to the laborious work of their unions. Without the unions, coal miners would be in worse shape than they are today, and maybe walking around looking more terrible than schoolteachers.

Coal miners are not represented in legislative bodies, either. In some states, lobbyists prevail; in other states, lobbyists barely exist. In the 1930s and 1940s, several political leaders from the East and Southeast paraded bills that were aimed at helping miners. They gained benefits that were considered the filet mignon of medical benefits.

Later, their efforts subsided, until now; further protections and recommended benefit packages are practically nonexistent and are often of bad hamburger quality. Attitudes toward coal miners have turned sour. Hillary Clinton ran for president and put up a dartboard with the faces of coal miners in her bathroom, right next to her toilet and high-security e-mail server.

Teachers, by comparison, eat filet mignon.

In every state, teachers belong to unions. In some states, teachers may opt out of formal union membership by paying an agency fee. Agency fees pose less of a financial strain than regular membership dues. But teachers who begrudgingly pay the fees and badmouth their union leaders—or teachers who belong to unions—profit from union benefits that aren't much different from those doled out to the agency fee group. Some teachers feel duped by compulsory union membership; they choose the cheapest route to travel.

Unions protect even the most antagonistic on the faculty. The more teachers tend to gripe about their professions, the more needy these teachers are of protections by teachers unions; at least, it seems that way.

In June of 2002, fifteen teachers met in a small barn in Musgrave, Texas.[30] Their mission: to figure out legal channels for dissolving their union and obliterating the collective bargaining process. No notes from this meeting have been found; no recordings were made. But from the information gathered, researchers have reconstructed part of the conversation that went on at this barnyard gathering. To simplify what may have been said during this conversation, we clump the plurality of teachers into the singular.

> LEADER: *Without these unions we'd have a better reputation.*
> TEACHER(S): *Reputation? Or decent salary and insurances?*
> LEADER: *We can have both.*
> TEACHER(S): *But how?*

LEADER: *That's why we're here: to figure that out.*
TEACHER(S): *We start with no membership fees or agency dues.*
LEADER: *How do we pass that sort of law?*
TEACHER(S): *We make it clear that unions screw teachers.*
LEADER: *They do?*
TEACHER(S): *Well, we know they screw the kids.*
LEADER: *They do? How?*
TEACHER(S): *Bad teachers are protected by tenure.*
LEADER: *But without tenure, you would have been fired years ago.*
TEACHER(S): *Okay. Right. I'll use myself as an example.*
LEADER: *Most teachers like unions. Nothing we say here will change that.*
TEACHER(S): *They know not what they do.*
LEADER: *Who are you? Jesus?*
TEACHER(S): *Most teachers don't have a clue.*
LEADER: *Yeah, imagine liking an organization that provides them higher salaries, equality protections, premium health benefits, and optimal job security. Yeah, they know not what they do.*
TEACHER(S): *And you know not what you say.*
LEADER: *Of course. This conversation, this meeting. It's nonsense.*
TEACHER(S): *Like the unions—nonsense.*
LEADER: *That's a non sequitur.*
TEACHER(S): *Non . . . what? I'm a teacher. I have no idea what that means.*

Lobbying efforts for teachers thrive. Strengths of these efforts vary by state; however, where they impact, they do some heavy-duty lifting. Most lobbyists in state capitals work in the trenches. They claw and clamor for money—not for themselves, but for education.

Salaries do go higher when bond issues and ballot propositions go through.[31] Money that has been earmarked, targeted, for specific programs or pet projects of educators or the general public frees up other money that may be used for salaries and fringe benefit packages. Unless you fix the leaky roof, you can't raise salaries. Fix the leaky roof with bonds, and you no longer have to give leaky-roof money to teachers.

Over four thousand *paid* education lobbyists work for teachers' interests.[32] Some of them toil nonstop. Unlike the coal miners, teachers have little chance of contracting a serious disease on the job, unless their arteries harden from all the prime rib they stuff down their gullets during some of those power lunches with state legislators.

Teachers have tough jobs. They are unfairly maligned. Often they are tragically attacked, their bodies and characters suffering the consequences of gossip and anonymous bashing and innuendo. Their health and welfare, at least to some extent, are in jeopardy while they work. They take home work they can't get done at school. Teachers organize, protest, and march together. They are often at each other's throats because they disagree over rudimentary questions that seemingly have no patented answers. Teachers don't make enough money on their own to support a family. They rarely receive medical benefits that they want to brag about.

But no matter how bad it gets for teachers, it ain't the coal mines.

NOTES

1. *October Sky*, directed by Joe Johnston, Universal Pictures, 1999.
2. Fossil fuels ran almost everything, including tanks and airplanes. Even sea vessels relied on the work of the miners. Wind power wouldn't have worked out so well. Wind power failed to do much good, even on wind chimes.
3. Pink Floyd, "Another Brick in the Wall (Part 2)," *The Wall*, 1979.
4. Melbourne Johnson, *American Homage* (Halpern, 1963), chapter 10.
5. The author found this survey on a memo that a school counselor gave to his English classes: "Most Marketable Skills: Your Best Chance to Get the Job You Really Deserve," a two-year study by the American Society for Research and Development, 1988. One may wonder why anybody deserves a particular job, just based on his *existence*. Perhaps, the reference here, though not clear, is if you possess these skills, you deserve a position at a Fortune 500 company.
6. According to a May 2014 report by Erika Rawes, Institute of the Future and the Bureau of Labor Statistics, the seven most marketable skills for the future are being adaptable, able to work on a virtual team, bilingual or multilingual, socially intelligent, cross-culturally adept, multidisciplinary, and analytical. Notice the significant differences in marketable skills from the 1988 report.
7. Bureau of Labor Statistics, "2015 National Industry-Specific Occupational Employment and Wage Statistics, NAICS 212100-Coal Mining," March 30, 2016, www.bls.gov/oes/current/naics4_212100.htm.
8. "5 Highest Paying States for Teachers," 2015, www.teachingmonster.com..
9. British Columbia Teachers' Federation, *BCTF Research Report*, July 2014. Teachers in the Northwest Territory make $118,000, although they have to travel about two hundred miles if they want a Big Mac.
10. Most salaries, when compared with those of doctors and lawyers, come out on the short end of the stick. But that's what some teachers do: they compare their salaries with salaries of other professions, those they have chosen not to enter.
11. No one in the profession worked harder than John. He rarely complained about money; he often complained about working conditions. These complaints were mostly about large class sizes, administrative failure in discipline follow-ups, and what he judged to be a lack of competency in some of his colleagues. John was about the kids. Administrators considered him a grumbler and troublemaker.
12. Bureau of Labor Statistics, "Occupational Unemployment Statistics," NAICS 212100–Coal Mining, March 30, 2016: compiled statistics.
13. John Spargo, *The Bitter Cry of Children* (New York: Macmillan, 1906), 163–65.
14. Ibid.
15. Allen Toussaint, "Working in a Coal Mine," 1981, lyrics.wikia.com/wiki/Allen_Toussaint:Working_In_The_Coal_Mine. Toussaint died in late 2015, at age seventy-seven.
16. *Bloomberg*, "The Deadliest Jobs in America," May 13, 2015, http://www.bloomberg.com/graphics/2015-dangerous-jobs/. These statistics were taken from a table indicating job fatalities for 2014. There was no specific teacher category. The statistics were compiled from categories of *educators*, *librarians*, and *training jobs*.
17. Anecdotal examples of teacher suicides exist. There are no recent statistics on teachers who would like to commit suicide but haven't gone through with it. Teachers reading this book may not wish to be counted in the next batch of statistics, however.
18. These are of the worst order. In 2016, in Placentia, California, a high school teacher hanged herself in her classroom. She made sure her students would find her early in the morning, which they did.

19. Richard Knight and Charlotte McDonald, "Do Those Who Retire Early Live Longer?" BBC News, July 23, 2012, http://www.bbc.co.uk/news/magazine-18952037.

20. *TES*, "The average age of death of a teacher...!?!?" February 23, 2004, https://community.tes.com/threads/statistics-the-average-age-of-death-of-a-teacher.148/

21. Those who detest experimental programs in our schools do so because they loathe the idea of using children as guinea pigs. Imagine that. Old folks who teach are less likely to try new things; thus, older teachers tend to bring parents a sense of security. Most parents want their children to feel safe at school. They want to know their children *are* safe at school. When parents discover a new program or module, even a novel scheduling scheme, they go berserk. At least some of them do. There is safety in the known, especially because so many new ideas have failed in such big ways. Safety, security: these are buzzwords. They have power and influence over the decision making of educators; unfortunately, too often, educators mistake what parents really want for something like putting up a fence around the shop area or serving grape tomatoes and garbanzo beans during lunches. Educators call these *safety* and *security*.

22. Robert Newsome, "Playing It through a Smile," *Methods in the Secondary School* (New York: Random House, 1963), 99–100.

23. The problem is that I can't figure out where this came from. But it is so well stated and powerful, I had to use it. I wouldn't have used it unless my other sources backed its accuracy, which they have, as indicated elsewhere in this chapter.

24. Norwalk-La Mirada Unified School District (California), salary schedule average, 2009–2016.

25. Going back to school to elevate positioning on the salary schedule is also a wonderful way for a teacher to take courses in areas that interest her. Most school districts allow for courses in any subject area that can be logically related to a subject taught in the schools: for example, a college class in criminology is easily applied to high school courses in social studies, civics, or the drug culture (which, admittedly, is not a high school class, but would help teachers in how to identify the stoners at the school).

26. Shaw's words were actually, "*Freedom* means responsibility" (italics added). But the same would hold true for *power*, a different word, but the same context. Anyway, it gets the point across: someone with a certain position has the flexibility (freedom) to exercise her power over others.

27. Norwalk-La Mirada Unified School District (California), typical benefits package, 2015.

28. The intent is to convince the employee to quit the district voluntarily. Teach a few classes in botany; that would do it. The teacher would run out of there in a minute.

29. Department for Professional Employees (DPE), "School Administrators: An Occupational Overview" Fact Sheet, 2014.

30. Hm-hm. Believe it or not. Hm-hm.

31. Some states do not allow bond measures to fund teachers' salaries; indirectly, bonds may fund teachers' salaries when they fund other programs. For example, a bond to build more classrooms passes; now, money in the general coffers is freed up to pay the district's teachers more money. Neat, how that works.

32. Joy Resmovits, "America's Education Reform Lobby Makes Its Presence Known At the Voting Booth," *The Huffington Post*, November 23, 2011, http://www.huffingtonpost.com/2011/11/21/education-reform-money-elections_n_1105686.html. Extrapolated.

Chapter Four

A Straw Man Named Tenure

In this age of the Internet, if a guy wants to denigrate someone, it's pretty easy to make stuff up and spread it around. A large body of people will hear about it—or read about it. It's not tough at all. Easy access to the Internet and other communication vehicles is the main reason people have to be particularly careful not to lie or be *mistaken* when they disseminate information or make accusations.

For a very long time, society extended de facto protections to its teachers. After all, teachers work with children. Children are our most precious commodities. Anybody instilled with that kind of responsibility—a *paid* responsibility, to boot—must be high on society's career chain. Thus, teachers are respected, admired, and protected.

At least, they *once* were.

The rumblings against teachers began in the 1950s when the Cold War got into full swing. Because Americans were now competing with the Russians—and to some extent, the Red Chinese—anybody retreating from his responsibility to compete, thus, thwarting America's ability to compete, was shunned.

Just how do teachers fit into the madness?

When America's students seemed to be lagging behind other nations' students in the 1950s, the blame for this academic plunge had to be placed somewhere. Up until then, people looked at the schools as an extension of the *Ozzie and Harriet* world they lived in; it was certainly a better school system in a number of different ways from the Little Red School House attended by America's pioneers' kids, or the "school room" they would call the back of a covered wagon. It took a while, but several wars and a few international crises finally awoke the American public: our schools could be doing better.

Our kids were struggling. Our pace to space was lagging. And our schools were sucking. It had to be *someone's* fault.

Bring on America's teachers.

Americans figured they were smart people. They also believed the teachers in America's schools were smart. But something was wrong. It did not connect. If teachers were smart, and if their students were no dumber than other countries' students, what was the problem?

Come on! There *had* to be something!

The "something" society came up with had little, or nothing, to do with the kids' abilities to learn. It had little, or nothing, to do with a teacher's knowledge of her subject matter, or her ability to impart her subject matter to her students. But it had *everything* to do with this: unqualified teachers keep their jobs. Bad teachers can't be fired. And why? *Tenure.* Or what they called *tenure*—and still do—even though "tenure" may not be exactly what people think it is.

How many times have you heard a parent say something like this about a teacher: "Mrs. Smith? She's awful! She shouldn't be teaching! She's so lazy! I can't believe *they can't fire her!*"?

The truth is they *can* fire her. Mrs. Smith may be fired after her first year of teaching. She may be fired in her thirtieth year of teaching. She may he booted after only two days of the school term. She may be canned by administrators at the school district, administrators at her school, or by a board of teachers and parents and students who perceive her to be incompetent, not fit to keep her job. She may be dismissed without that job protection known as *tenure*.

Or she may be released under the protections of tenure. Those who think tenure is a foolproof method of shielding bad teachers in order to keep them in the system, while hurting children, are dead wrong.

Period.

End of issue: well, unfortunately, not quite end of issue. The best way to approach this is to describe what educators (and the public) mean when they speak of tenure . . . and what tenure really is, in *fact*.

In education, perceptions have become *everything. Encarta® World English Dictionary* defines *perception*: "quick to understand or discern things or show understanding of a person or a situation." In other words, a particular perception swims in the eye of the beholder. If you think it's true, it stands as the reality (until another time, when that "reality" can be altered through the acceptance of a fact—or yet another perception).

Perceptions used to be easily dismissed. No matter what the industry or activity, if someone held a particular perception about something, and that perception was off base, completely out of touch with reality, he was corrected. Eventually, the original perception faded, transmogrifying, perhaps, into another reality.

People were susceptible to changing their minds, altering their discernment of right and wrong, or even facts. They still are. But because in the last several decades opinions have been chased by perceptions, and opinions are revered in some circles as synonymous to statements of facts, opinions have carried a lot more weight than they used to, almost to the point of becoming reality.

Teachers and teacher unions have been maligned for their tenure policies. But the truth is . . . *most people have gotten it all wrong*! Their perceptions are inaccurate—in a *big* way!

The objective truth—not a *perception*— about tenure: *there is no such thing as tenure*. What the public and politicians have spoken of in pejorative terms as *tenure* does not exist. What does exist is *due process* for people who work in education, especially teachers. The idea that after a given point, a teacher can't be fired is *absolutely not true*! In fact, teachers *have* been fired for various reasons. But they have not been dismissed willy-nilly, based on a parent's or an administrator's whim—or because on a given day a principal had a stick up his you-know-what.

There have been cases where a horrible teacher has continued to teach; there have been instances where an excellent teacher has been railroaded out of a school. But these are exceptions to the rule.[1]

Individuals who are afforded *due process* rights in their contracts have greater job security than people hired by the local Walmart. The Walmart boss can pull the trigger at any moment. The Walmart boss can fire an employee with little protocol, or determine the proper protocol on the spur of the moment. But to be fair: Americans want the average guy or gal to have some protections while on the job. They want it for themselves, and they want it for others, too. It is only right. And humane.

It's smart, too. Workers who toil in careers in which they have to walk a tightrope every day contract anxieties that make their job performance worse. Teachers are no different. In order for teachers to work at their peak, in a job that has a direct effect on the health and well-being of kids, they should know the principal isn't going to immediately visit them in their classrooms with armed guards ready to escort them from the school grounds because an irate parent complained about their classroom seating arrangement.

However—and this is a big *however*—children and the public demand, and deserve, protections, too. Despite what people hear about the tenure system, the children and public receive those protections.

Teachers who flunk out usually have no place to go for gainful employment. They can't get a real job; in fact, in the beginning when they were first searching for a job or deciding what it was they wanted to do with their lives, they may have discovered that they were incapable of doing *anything* else. The teaching profession let them enter during a particularly ripe period for teachers and education; they didn't have to screw in a light bulb or fix a leaky pipe. So once they had toiled away inside the system for two or three years, they received a form of job security in education known as *tenure*.

Contrary to popular myth, tenure doesn't mean a teacher can't be fired for *anything*. It also doesn't mean that once teachers have been at a school or in the same district long enough, they are guaranteed permanence. "Tenure" is really due process; it's a prescribed procedure that the employer (the school district) is required by law to go through in order to get rid of an employee (the teacher) for cause.

For the purpose of clarification, here are the basics of tenure:

1. Tenure is *due process*; it is not immunity from job dismissal.
2. Private schools do not have to grant tenure; the vast majority do not.
3. Most public schools have some form of tenure.
4. Tenure laws vary by state and by district, and they are changing all the time.
5. The courts have upheld the legality of teacher tenure.
6. The average length of time for a teacher to receive tenure in a school district is from two to three years; most teachers receive tenure after their second year in a district.
7. Tenure is a guarantee of employment in a particular school district, not a specific school.
8. Tenure is unique to faculty; administrators and noncertificated staff do not receive tenure.
9. Teachers may be hired on a nontenure track; that is, at their contract signing, they agree to wait an *additional* probationary period before entering a two- or three-year traditional probationary period. After that time, they may be granted tenure.
10. Most parents would like to tell educators they should take their tenure policies and make them history.

That said, state tenure laws have protected some dreadful teachers; it's become extremely difficult to fire horrible educators. Teacher buyouts have become popular. Bad teachers have been brought to court before old, disgruntled judges who wished that they had "tenure," too.

But everyone should stand back a moment. Political leaders and community activists, along with well-intentioned parents, who have been wholly critical of tenure protections for teachers, are woefully short of substantial statistical evidence that supports the destruction of schools because of tenure. *Absolutely,* anecdotal examples of poor teachers and their unwarranted longevity in education exist. Much to the dismay of educators—*especially* educators—these isolated horror stories have polluted the hearts and minds of anyone, and everyone, who even *thinks* about the effectiveness of America's schools, and the welfare of America's children.

Obviously, education is still a state function. Despite Common Core and International Baccalaureate (IB) and other, minor, silly one-world programs that have popped up, the federal government still designates the individual states to run their own schools. This is one of the main reasons why so many schools lag.

State variations in learning philosophies, values, reverence for education, and economics have turned education into a game kids play called "The Luck of the Draw." Or, to be accurate: if you're a child who lives in a state that cares about schools and children learning what *truly* matters, you are extremely lucky. If you're a child born in a state that has established a warped sense of priorities for spending money, and believes school curriculum should be geared to a one-size-fits-all agenda, you are extremely *un*lucky.

In that regard, a few states have abolished the bulk of their due-process protections for teachers. Others have watered them down a bit. Some have confused the scenario by spewing loads of modern verbiage and political goop no normal person can decipher.

However—and *this is big*—the prevalent viewpoint on due-process protections is that these protections do a lot more good than harm. While there will continue to be reappraisals on the state of teacher job protections in the United States, politicians and parents should remember that teacher shortages have been cyclically rampant in this country: they come and go. When they *come*, it is difficult to get good people into the schools. Most of the good people want real jobs where they tend to earn real money. Without job security, no one will want to teach. Who can blame them?

Job protections should be fair and reasonable. Not a single child should be sacrificed for a teacher's holding onto a position at a school. The system should reflect such a tendency. But America's teachers should not be sacrificial lambs in a system that knits a fabric of conspiratorial scapegoating against its educators.

If you listen to some, *nothing* would replace teacher tenure. Public school teachers do not warrant more protections than those received by employees in the private sector.[2] And this opinion is shared by many: a recent poll reported that 45 percent of *teachers* and 72 percent of the general public would vote for an initiative that invoked a law that forbade (these) teacher job protections from being a substantial part of the collective bargaining process.[3]

In other words, except for the unions, Americans hate teacher job-security laws.

Most adults today lived in an era when teachers were revered. The word "rabbi," for example, means *teacher*. A rabbi is the ultimate teacher—and God is his principal.

Okay, maybe not. Perhaps, that's an exaggeration or a mixed metaphor. But you get the point: Jews have respected teachers to the hilt over the years;

yet American Jews are at the forefront of the protests to "please do something about teacher tenure!"[4] This may also say something about how much they like the rabbis at their own synagogues. But in all likelihood, it simply means that American Jews, like other religious and ethnic groups in the United States, view American education as going to hell;[5] they have taken the easy way out and assigned most of this demise to their perceived failures of their children's teachers.

This certainly seems like an incongruence, doesn't it? All the respect afforded to teachers; all the holy adulation directed toward teachers. So what gives? Why does the public clamor for laws that make it easier to fire teachers?

Yes, I love teachers! Yes, our teachers are the chosen few who have been selected to help God do His work: to mold the lives of our children. Bless them! Bless our teachers! They have risen to the occasion by their participation in the most challenging of all professions!

By the way, let's make their lives riddled with ambiguities and insecurities by eliminating their job security protections.

So, to answer the original question: What should/would replace current "tenure" policies? Most states have declared *nothing*. They have kept the laws the way they are, or they have thrown a blanket over tenure, waiting to see if there will continue to be a teacher surplus—with *anybody* and his distant, long-lost cousin willing to take a teaching job—or a teacher shortage, before they declare what to do about altering teacher tenure laws.

Before reading this short list of what some states have already done about tenure, keep in mind that change should be beneficial and commensurate with the needs to make those changes. Change for the sake of change is usually not good. Change based solely on public clamoring and political ignorance is even worse:

Dozens of states have changed their tenure laws in the last few years. The Education Commission of the States found that as of 2011, eighteen states had modified their tenure laws. And that trend continues.

In 2011, Florida eliminated continuing contracts for teachers. South Dakota got rid of tenure for new hires but will grandfather those hired until 2016 into the previous tenure system. Idaho gave school districts the option of forgoing tenure, but voters overturned that decision in a referendum.

The Education Commission of the States keeps a database on its website to inform teachers, parents, administrators, and legislators of changes and the status of lawsuits related to education.

In 2012, Louisiana governor Bobby Jindal spearheaded a sweeping reform to the state education system, which would make it harder to earn and retain tenure. In October, the Louisiana Supreme Court upheld the proposed changes to the Louisiana teacher-tenure law.[6]

Do legislators understand what tenure really is?

Here is what tenure is *not*. It is not a guaranteed job for life. You (the teacher) have passed a probationary period of time and now you must be given a substantiated reason before you can be fired. By the way, you can be fired/dismissed at any point in your career. But some legislators—and school districts—prefer to fire at will and without reason. Too bad we can't do that with politicians. Most people would like to evaluate their local councilman's proficiency. Students' test scores measure teachers' effectiveness? Let's measure politicians' effectiveness based on their ability to make sense and tell the truth.

Recently, a teacher in Los Angeles was suspended because a physics lesson about motion involved equipment (not a weapon) that *looked* like a weapon. It was a wrench. Schools across the nation have made marshmallow "guns," rail accelerators, and model rockets.[7] What is the world coming to?

Teachers shouldn't be fired because they teach evolution, *Catcher in the Rye*, algebra's Islamic origins, the McCarthy era—or use models that resemble weapons in science experiments.

Do we want teachers to give honest grades, enforce school codes, and make difficult choices? How soon until teachers are fired for giving an "A−" instead of an "A" grade? Maybe a teacher complains about a student's deplorable conditions at home, or abuse, and is terminated for making waves? Teachers must make unpopular decisions and advocate for students against powerful forces. Without due process, learning may be sacrificed for politics.

California's teachers were in danger of losing tenure protections due to a major court decision. Even before a judge's scathing ruling against California's teacher-tenure laws, the once-sacred protections that make it harder to fire teachers already had been weakened in many states, and even removed altogether in some places.[8]

Kansas and North Carolina also are seeking to eliminate tenure, or phase it out. The nonpartisan Education Commission of the States, which highlighted the changes in a report mentioned earlier, says sixteen states—up from ten in 2011—now require the results of teacher evaluations be used in determining whether to grant tenure.[9]

Not all changes have stuck, and few are without a political fight.

Teacher-tenure protections were established in the twentieth century to save teachers from arbitrary or discriminatory firings based on factors such as gender, nationality, or political beliefs. They spell out rules under which teachers may be dismissed after they pass a probationary period.

Critics say the tenure protections make it too difficult to fire ineffective teachers.

The debate over teacher tenure comes as many states, propelled by Obama administration–led incentives, develop more meaningful teacher evaluation systems that seek to provide a more accurate picture of student learning under a teacher. Using such systems, the Education Commission of the States says seven states make teachers return to probationary status if they are rated "ineffective," meaning they have no assurances their contracts will be renewed at the end of the school year.

Michelle Exstrom, education program director at the National Conference of State Legislatures, says, "A number of states have effectively done away with tenure through their new evaluation systems that include measurements of student achievement."[10]

Los Angeles Superior Court judge Rolf Treu sided with nine wise students who sued to overturn California statutes governing teacher hiring and firing. The students argued that these statutes served no compelling purpose and had led to an unfair, nonsensical system that drove excellent new teachers from the classroom too soon. Incompetent senior teachers, on the other hand, were kept.[11] These practices harm students in a way that "shocks the conscience" and have "a disproportionate burden on poor and minority students," the judge wrote.[12]

While the ruling affects only California, proponents of rolling back tenure protections say the landscape is ripe for change. They predict the judge's ruling will spur a flood of new legislative action and more lawsuits. They say that K–12 teachers merely have to show up for work for a set period of time to earn tenure protection.[13]

That's the case in thirty-one states, according to the National Council on Teacher Quality. Sandi Jacobs, a vice president from the organization, who testified in the California case on behalf of the plaintiffs, said tenure protections for teachers aren't necessarily a bad thing, but obtaining tenure status should be meaningful, and due process should be reasonable. Jacobs said California is one of a small number of states that requires seniority to be used in making lay-off decisions.[14]

Randi Weingarten, president of the American Federation of Teachers union, argued that taking away due-process rights ultimately hurts low-income schools because teachers won't want to take a risk teaching in such schools without strong labor protections.[15]

Due process allows good teachers to "take risks on behalf of their kids," Weingarten said.

Dennis Van Roekel, president of the National Education Association, which also represents teachers, says the tenure fight is a distraction that takes away from other important education issues. He says school districts need to focus on hiring practices. "I think there ought to be a system to dismiss bad teachers. It ought to be fair to the employer and employee, and it ought to be cost-effective, but it should be used very rarely," Van Roekel said. "Because if you have a system where that number is high, there's something wrong with your recruitment and hiring."[16]

In states where teacher tenure has been rolled back, Van Roekel observed that teachers have reacted negatively because "they are afraid and they fear bad things will happen to good people."[17]

Robert Pianta, dean of the Curry School of Education at the University of Virginia, said that in California and elsewhere, more is known about who is a good teacher in this age of annual (robust) testing of students. He said he believes this so-called knowledge spurred the California lawsuit and other movement on the issue. He predicts more states will move toward longer probationary periods to grant tenure and more renewable contracts.[18]

But even as state lawmakers debate the issue, not all are moving forward with change.

New Jersey governor Chris Christie has finished assaulting Marco Rubio and is working hard to reform the tenure system in New Jersey. He does not want to eliminate the tenure system completely. He wants to extinguish the current tenure system and replace it with a new one.[19]

Currently, in New Jersey, after a teacher proves himself efficient for three years, he gains lifetime protection under tenure. Christie wants teachers to work for three years to gain tenure. But after one year of being deemed "ineffective," teachers may easily be fired. Christie advocates a two-part assessment. One part of the score will be based on student achievement. A second part of the score will be based on teacher performance. Christie believes the answer to making schools more effective is to place more accountability on teachers. He said, "Let New Jersey lead the way again. The time to eliminate teacher tenure is now."[20]

The primary purpose of this book is to defend America's teachers. Yes, there are several areas of concern. And there are those places in which America's teachers are clearly indefensible. But much of the drama coming from the public and, particularly, the leadership of both major political parties, is blind rhetoric in the guise of truth.

Here's the bottom-line knowledge on tenure:

1. Teacher tenure is an easy target. Any system that, supposedly, offers such (perceived) grandiose job security would be an easy target. Most Americans live year to year, month to month—even week to week or day-to-day—in a state of flux concerning the stability of their employment. *How nice it must be to go to a job from which you may not be fired.*

2. Even with tenure, a teacher *may* be fired. While tenure—so-called tenure—promises due process, incompetent teachers are fired all the time (varies by state), and the kind of job security that people *perceive* is not truly in existence.

3. In order for the bulk of our educational ills to be tied to teacher tenure, other causal relationships have to be made. An inability to fire teachers contributes to the fact that bad teachers continue forever on the job, which equals poor test scores, unsavory physical conditions at the various school

sites, corrupt administrators, children coming to school who are unwilling to learn or incapable of learning, overcrowded classrooms, drug and alcohol abuse among the nation's students, dropout rates, dwindling budgets, neglectful or abusive parents . . . and, really, the list goes on and on and on. Trying to draw correlations to tenure would be a ridiculous, wasteful endeavor.

4. In several places where tenure has been perceived to be damaging, there have been movements underfoot to abolish or significantly alter tenure policies. Some of these movements and pieces of legislation may be laudable. Time will judge. So far, little significance—or relevance—can be ascertained from new policies.

5. The basic premise that there are thousands of unsavory, inept, incompetent teachers working in America's classroom is inaccurate; it is condescending, patronizing. More than anything, it is downright offensive. When bad cops shoot disarmed or unarmed victims, the bad cops should be dealt with. When bad plumbers damage homes, they should be dealt with. When bad teachers show a recurrent ineptness, they should be dealt with. When people paint all, or even a majority, of these individuals with a broad stroke of the same brush, it demonstrates impatience, ignorance, or—sorry to say this outright—blatant stupidity on the part of the people who are handling that brush.[21]

Teacher tenure may be a good thing; it may be a bad thing. Some teachers deserve to teach their entire lives, reaping the rewards of their chosen profession; other teachers should not spend even another day inside a classroom. What ails American education can't be remedied by scaring old teachers into an early retirement, discouraging budding new, talented teachers away from the profession, or even dismissing the few who are truly awful educators.

America's preoccupation with tenure must not turn the public's collective attention from where it really belongs.

NOTES

1. "Evaluating Good and Bad Teaching," *Faculty Herald* (Temple University) 44, no. 2. Hardly anyone in authority actually makes this statement. I believe there are more good teachers than bad teachers. But this is unquantifiable, so we have to extrapolate from this source and others, as well.

2. "Why Do Teachers Deserve Tenure?" Daily Kos, June 12, 2014, http://www.dailykos.com/story/2014/6/12/1306416/-Why-Do-Teachers-Deserve-Tenure.

3. Ibid. I inferred this from trends in the data. The percentage may be off one or two points in either direction. But the overall sentiment is not in doubt. People do not like teacher-tenure laws.

4. This is, of course, another weak attempt at humor.

5. The support for my speculation here is lacking, although I did find a lot of information about Jews who believe other Jews are going to hell for enjoying cheeseburgers (a lie, because Jews don't believe in the concept of hell).

6. Will Sentell, "Radical Changes to Louisiana Public Schools," *The Advocate*, June 15, 2015, http://theadvocate.com/news/12728536-123/jindal-topples-status-quo-in.

7. "Teacher Shows Kids Carpentry Tools, Gets Suspended on Weapons Charge," *Free-Range Kids*, April 22, 2014, http://www.freerangekids.com/teacher-shows-kids-carpentry-tools-gets-suspended-on-weapons-charge.

8. Rebecca Klein, "Confused as to Where to Stand on Teacher Tenure?" Huffington Post, August 12, 2014, http://www.huffingtonpost.com/2014/08/12/teachers-unions-yougov-poll_n_5669090.html.

9. Ibid.

10. Michelle Exstrom, "Do Teachers Make the Grade?" *State Legislatures Magazine*, December 2013, http://www.ncsl.org/research/education/do-teachers-make-the-grade.aspx.

11. Howard Blume and Stephen Ceasar, "California Teacher and Seniority System Is Struck Down," *Los Angeles Times*, June 10, 2014, Local Education, 1.

12. Ibid.

13. In July of 2016, California tenure protection was upheld by a higher court.

14. Howard Blume and Stephen Ceasar, "California Teacher and Seniority System Is Struck Down," *Los Angeles Times*, June 10, 2014, Local Education, 1.

15. Ibid.

16. Eric Westervelt, "From Calif. Teachers, More Nuanced View on Tenure," *nprED*, June 10, 2014, http://www.npr.org/sections/ed/2014/07/10/329533444/from-calif-teachers-more-nuanced-views-on-tenure.

17. Ibid.

18. "Teacher Protections Weakened Even before Hillary Ruling," CBS News, June 12, 2014, http://www.cbsnews.com/news/teacher-tenure-protections-weakened-before-california-judges-ruling/.

19. Kate Zernike, "Chris Christie Signs Bill Overhauling Job Guarantees for Teachers," *New York Times*, August 6, 2012, NY/Region, 1.

20. Ibid.

21. Ironically, this may one of the best arguments *against* teacher tenure. Teacher reviews and evaluations are individually based. They take into consideration a teacher's strengths and weaknesses, just the opposite of the "broad brush" approach.

Chapter Five

Not a Teacher's Friend

Most educators spend more time administering tests to their students than they do actually teaching them the subject matter in their courses.[1]

In addition to tests mandated by the class curriculum, there are state-sponsored tests, federally mandated tests, locally required tests, and optional department tests. Students also face those annoying tests that don't seem to have a rhyme or reason behind them, such as career-aptitude tests and morals/ethics tests.

The first sentence of this chapter doesn't tell the truth. The endnote explains this, but not every reader immediately bounces over to the endnotes page. The reason for this hyperbole: teachers, directly or indirectly, are responsible for too many time-consuming tests, some of which lead to inaccurate diagnoses, and many of which are downright counterproductive.

Teachers are *indirectly* responsible, because of their complicity: after all, teachers administer the exams, usually in their classrooms. Teachers are *directly* responsible for these tests, because they (at least, many teachers) actually agree with the system that conspires to maintain this policy.

Among those teachers that despise testing, few publicly criticize the policy; even fewer report to the channels (administrators, community leaders, politicians) that have power to make changes. This is why teachers are complicit, either directly or indirectly, in the tedious, wasteful, and counterproductive testing process.

Rachael Minton, the (so-called) assessment coordinator in a large suburban school district, commented in 2014, "Testing is just one more thing that our teachers complain about. . . . [Teachers] direct their criticisms of the testing process at me, because I am in the unenviable position of having to supervise the accountability and assessment policies in [our district]. . . . If [teachers] really wanted to see their complaints have some impact, they would complain to the right people."[2]

Who are the "right people," Ms. Minton? And where might they be found? Obviously, they are not *you*: if schools were to trim the standardized testing process, you would be out of a job. The bureaucracy would dwindle. Money—lots and lots of money—would be saved. In fact, Ms. Minton, your six-figure salary could be used to hire two additional teachers, men and women who preside inside an actual classroom and teach kids about things you would no longer be around to assess them on. Teachers who currently can't get jobs because of dwindling allocations and stricter budgets may be able to land a classroom of their own and teach students in environments where classroom sizes are manageable.

Wonderful, huh? And possible, if you (and many others like you) lost *your* jobs.

Ragging on administrations is not something to be taken lightly; in fact, criticism of administrators should be kept to a minimum. Administrators are not primary culprits. It's fashionable to complain about site and district administrators simply because they *exist*. But that's not their fault. All people would like to exist. Nobody wants to lose her job. The focus should be on the *quality* of a district administrator, and what that individual does to the psyche of teachers, students, and, ultimately, the general public.

Putting a high-salaried person in charge of assessment says a lot for the significance of assessment—or, at least, it should. But exactly how much of a statement about the importance of testing children in school until they have Scantrons and bubble sheets coming out their noses should be made? After all, politicians and the general public are already listening. And watching. To most of these people, testing is the Holy Grail. They bow to testing. They sing the praises of Scantrons and bubble sheets. They grovel in the presence of assessment coordinators.

Clearly, educators have to test students' progress: in their individual classes, their various subjects, and even their comparative (to the rest of the world) progress. But enough is enough. There's a point of the absurd. Everything can't be about a test. Humanity is lost. Self-worth is lost. Time is lost. And because some cultures make testing (and school in general) the be-all and end-all for their children, even *lives* are lost.

Perhaps, one aspect of testing that vanishes in the fracas is the effect the current testing rage has on teachers. It's brutal, man. Teachers have lives and families and souls. If the significance of testing, considering the extent the schools utilize this process, proves somewhat beneficial, the sacrifice of lives and families and souls may be argued to be worth it when it comes to an overall cost/benefit analysis. But it's not. Testing stinks. Testing is not the teacher's friend.

Over-Testing

The term *over-testing* implies that the education system tests students too much, more than they should test students. This problem alone—only if it were *alone*—would be bad enough. But when you also consider the other drawbacks of testing, combined with a newfound realization that students are tested far beyond the boundaries of reasonability, every other consequence to the testing process stands out as exponentially worse than already thought.

Those other drawbacks come next; for now, ponder what we are doing to the children in our schools under the guise of reasonable assessment practices (which consist of failures ultimately blamed on teachers).

Testing overlaps. Bridget Wasserman, California State University education professor, observed, "The right hand rarely knows what the left hand is doing . . . for the right hands doesn't *care* [italics added] what the left hand is doing."[3]

If various assessment coordinators actually considered the different modes of assessment inundation, they would do a much better job of, well, *coordinating*. But they don't. Or won't. When a state schedules *achievement* exams at the end of the school term, it's not a cogent idea to test the same kids for another exam at, basically, the same time. Those who take five or six days of achievement tests must concurrently tend to their state-standards exam (a different test, usually with, sadly, a remarkable amount of redundancy). The standards exam also can run for a couple of days, challenging our kids to maintain even a semblance of their sanity for the duration of the testing schedule.

Next comes proficiency testing, but with a twist.

The twist is . . . there is no twist. Naturally, most students expect something a little different by the time they get to their third or fourth standardized test, but they usually get the same *Read the passage and answer the questions.* Here the challenge for students, whether they are in grade eleven or grade four, is to stay awake while they are reading those passages. No matter how you mix the recipe or cook the concoction, when you are sitting day after day at a hard desk in a stuffy classroom, you don't give a rat's behind about odd extra-planetary occurrences or osmosis in wild plants. All you want to do is fill in those bubbles with some degree of accuracy and then escape to the nearest bathroom before you wet your pants.

Add to these tests the stock exams that all K–12 students take each and every school term, honors tests, AP tests, graduation proficiency tests, and International Baccalaureate tests, and it's no wonder kids are running to stress pills, marijuana plants, and therapy sessions in order to control their irritable bowel syndrome.[4]

Not to be overlooked or forgotten: teacher-administered course tests. Final exams are big in school, especially in the upper grades. But the chief blunder is that the geniuses who have "coordinated" these major standardized state- and district-sponsored tests have tossed them into the mix around the same time as the subject exams, perpetrating the feeling among many children that they have died and gone to hell (or been forced to watch several hours of a political convention).

But even the subject exams overlap: Haven't you heard of a student facing a math final, a science final, and a Spanish final on the same day? Sometimes these come on the heels of those dreaded, excruciating AP exams.

Consider the large number of tests students are apt to take during a single school year. Think about how this multitude of tests is likely to cause overlap and redundancy, much less permit our children an opportunity to *learn* anything before, or after, they have run the gamut of testing:

- state standards exams (5 to 7 days, usually once a year)
- graduation proficiency (exit) exams (around 3 days, repeated as necessary)
- IQ tests (2 or 3 times, usually in grade school, and as necessary)
- AP, honors, GATE (qualification exams—*3 times* for GATE)
- Advanced Placement tests (4 or 5 subjects, at least 1 day for each)
- proficiency tests (4 times per year: in math and English)
- career aptitude tests (several times during a student's school career)
- course subjects (teacher administered) exams (frequently)
- course final exams (all subjects, once per semester: high school, middle school)
- college entrance exams (takes 1 day but requires hours, days, weeks of prep)

Each state has its own sets of exam schedules. Some states have more exams in the elementary schools than they do in the upper grades, and in other states, the reverse is true: the upper grades are more test loaded than the lower grades. But any way you look at it, it's tests *galore*.

Private schools, as a rule, have more latitude than public schools do when it comes to testing, but they still have to cater to stringent standards established by colleges and universities. It is to the financial advantage of a private institution to keep testing to a minimum.

And private schools require fewer assessment coordinators.

The bottom line: schools test too much; schools test too often. Besides creating havoc and a general sense of confusion among teachers and students, the current testing situation thwarts the main reason kids are in schools and teachers are in their classrooms: to learn.

Needless Anxiety

Occasionally, it's good for you to remember you were once a child—and how you felt about that awful affliction. Recollections of your past, especially those from during the time you spent in the hallowed halls of academic institutions, may serve a practical dose of nostalgia: if the remembrances are particularly ugly, you try to blot them out, to ignore them, or to view them as the successes they were *not*. But those memories are there. They aren't going anywhere, either. Why not use them to your advantage, rather than as barriers to understanding what's really wrong with our schools?

If educators took the time to remember how they felt about things when they were in school (much less, how they now feel as teachers), they would make better decisions about what's best for students today—what's best for kids, in general.

Test anxiety was never a good thing for you. The guilt you felt for doing something else besides studying for an important exam was enough to make you want to crawl into a hole. You knew there were too many times you had preferred to see a movie, watch a ballgame, or hang out with your friends instead of spending time cooped up in your room studying the Periodic Elements Table, your head stilled, nostrils flared, under the glare of a bright white light. And so you didn't study. You had fun instead. Even if you had somehow managed to ace that exam, the stress you experienced from not laboring over our notes and books—or *because* you had labored over our notes and books—did not equate to a fair price for your horrendous testing experience. Just what would have happened if you had scored a B+ on the geometry test instead of an A-? Or a C instead of a B? Who would have died?

Classroom stresses are further compounded by state- and federally mandated testing, thus bringing our kids to a new level of stress. Some teachers have told their students (regarding state standards testing): "Do *whatever you have to do* in order to get the highest score you can. Keeping your house may depend on it."

The reference here is to values of houses in the neighborhood. The prices of homes largely depend upon the desirability of a neighborhood. And the desirability of the neighborhood provides a direct indicator of the quality of the schools in that neighborhood. The way society currently measures the quality of a school is by how high its students score on tests: low scores equate to crappy schools. And crappy schools equate to stinky neighborhoods. When it comes down to it, who wants to pay a high price for a house in a stinky neighborhood?[5]

So, Kevin, you had better do a good job on your tests! If you do not, here's hoping your parents don't have to sell their house!

Talk about pressure! Some children believe their ability to add and subtract accurately dictates whether or not they are going to have a place to sleep at night.

Okay, hyperbole. But undue—and it *is* undue—stress thrust upon our nation's schoolchildren ought to be significantly curtailed. When it comes right down to it, educators should be ashamed of themselves for not having fixed this problem.

Teachers wind up taking the brunt of the stress implosion.

While it is absolutely true that some of our teachers are worse than mediocre and could not, to use a hackneyed expression, teach their way out of a wet paper bag, the (newly created) *institution* of testing in our schools has brought along an entirely different level of stress for teachers. It's worse than bad: a phenomenon that highly educated (often brilliant) men and women are at a loss to explain crawls insidiously into the very fabric of a teacher's life. It is crucial that the general public understands the tremendous impact testing has on the teachers of America.

Extortion prevails. That's a loaded word. But here's its justification: *extortion* is blackmail. Blackmail is when you threaten to do something bad to another person if she doesn't comply with your wishes. If the principal of a middle school calls Mrs. Jalapeño into her office and makes a threatening statement, it might be extortion. Consider the following (sample) statement from a high school principal and decide whether or not you find this to be a form of blackmail: *Mrs. Jalapeño, your students (in your English class) had very low reading scores on last year's standards exam. I am expecting your classes' scores to go up by at least 10 percent this year; if they do not, I am assigning you to teach dumbbell English next semester.*

The term *dumbbell English* is no longer used—at least, not publicly. And not formally; however, being demoted from teaching the so-called cream of the crop and then dumped into a classroom full of children who haven't done a homework assignment or passed a test since the Chicago Cubs last won the World Series[6] is clearly a job downgrade. Or worse: the principal might threaten the teacher with the loss of her job if her students do not perform better on their next batch of state-sponsored tests.

Does the flagrant warning of a demotion or firing sound like extortion? Hmm . . . ?

There are those who defend a system that punishes teachers for not bringing their students along to the Promised Land on their standardized tests. They contend it is the teacher's job to teach, to make certain her students learn all there is to learn; the students then must perform on the tests and the teacher held accountable for her students' performances.

The stress level placed on students and teachers is at a new high. It is difficult to measure and quantify degrees of stress; it is similarly difficult to determine quantifiable consequences related to stress (that have been caused by testing). An objective determination of these factors is practically impossible. The next best thing is to lean on qualified experts who have well-supported opinions on this subject: Harton Ramsey noted that in South Korea (and in Japan), the suicide rates among secondary students have risen in the last twenty years. Notable attempts to determine the catalysts for these tragic events have harkened experts *back to the school* and the students' home environment.[7]

Children who have a difficult time adjusting to a social environment have a monstrous time finding any affability in their school experience. And then what happens? Sinking into the hardcore nature of a curriculum can be daunting. Without a more pleasant distraction or involvement for the student in a direction that best suits her needs, trouble looms. . . . This trouble may take the form of an academic crash . . . or worse.

Bottom line: students do not find taking tests fun. What's different now is that kids don't find academics fun, either (which they hardly ever do—or did); they are no longer being distracted by more suitable interactions on school grounds or at home. As parents, teachers, peers, and society place more and more pressure on children to succeed in school, the children's anxiety rates soar. And the effects of that anxiety are crippling: more testing, more stress, more consequences.

Lots of kids have bragged about scoring near perfect on their SATs (or, more likely, their *parents* have bragged). But at what price? And to what end?

Wasting Time

Worth repeating: as a concept, testing students in order to gauge accurately their achievement is a *good* thing. The concepts of evaluation and assessment have been around longer than sliced bread (or peanut butter). The indictment of testing hasn't to do with the nature of testing—or its value in the educational process; it *has* to do with five factors: (1) its overuse, (2) its redundancy, (3) its inflated importance, (4) its negative impact on teachers, and (5) its negative impact on students.

This list of common complaints about testing was gathered from several teachers who were interviewed for this project.[8] These teachers were encouraged to speak honestly and freely—and they did:

> Rather than painting the whole picture for my students—a method by which they would learn a lot more from me—I am forced to break my subject matter down into much smaller increments [units]. This is a way of teaching that I don't like because it stalls the curriculum and confuses students.
>
> I understand the viability of testing, but when we test so often, the students learn less. I didn't get my degree in test administration; I got it in history. I

want to use my classroom time wisely; I have this crazy notion that actually teaching history in a history class is the best possible use of my students' and my time.

Giving redundant tests is what bothers me the most. I'm a language arts [English] teacher, so we often assess my students' reading levels. If I take the time to do this in class, I don't see why the school has to do it again, and then the district—through state mandates or whatever—has to do these tests a third or fourth time. It's rather maddening.

My students have become test drunk. They are only in the third grade! I quiz my students in my own way [usually fun, pain free] in order to find out what they have learned, but then representatives from our school district come in and do it again. And near the end of each school year I must announce to my eight-year-olds that they are going to be tested again, this time by the state of California. I have to make up this long spiel about how important it is that we do this so many times and—Lord help me!—how good it is to participate in this wonderful process, one that is looking out for them and their welfare! It pains me to be such a liar to the children who trust me the most.

Some of the older teachers who have not yet retired lament about bygone days when a teacher could still be a teacher. She could teach what she thought was important, using her professional judgment; then she could (and this is crucial) *evaluate the aptitude of her class and decide what she needed to adjust so they might learn better*. She might reteach the whole unit; repeat certain concepts that were particularly difficult for her students; administer a *test* to check her students' progress or to assess what they learned; give the test again (or a similar test); or do other evaluative procedures, such as small group projects, oral presentations, summary papers, or whole class projects. What's more, the teacher might decide not to do anything at the end of the teaching process. Perhaps, she was already satisfied with the way her students responded to her lessons, how hard they worked, or their degree of enthusiasm. As a reward for her students, she could waive the assessment process altogether, put on a film, and order a pizza.

Puzzling Thoughts

The *right* reason to test, of course, is to find out how much the students have learned. Their progress is judged in an assortment of academic subjects, elective areas and activity courses and through cumulative assessments done by and state and federal agencies. The extent educators and government officials *do* something with test results could determine their viability and, perhaps, a need for more (gulp!) testing.

Usually, the media disclose the scores of state achievement tests. Scores are always reported to local school sites. Results are given to the parents of the students who take the tests. The children never get to see their scored tests so they rarely know which problems they got wrong.

And then what happens remains a mystery.

Some school administrators call teachers for meetings; they go over their department's test results and try to figure out what those results mean. Occasionally, the teachers identify problems the kids had a particularly difficult time with and vow to do something to correct the nonlearning that has apparently taken place.

Unfortunately, what works successfully for one teacher does not work well for another teacher; what may work to postpone the demise of one student may not work to save another student. Unless Hitler is running the teachers' meetings, the teachers compromise. They come to the understanding that each teacher's autonomy is crucial, that if they are to improve as teachers, and their students are going to banish what plagues them, teachers will do it in their own way, using their professional judgment as to what needs to be done.

Kevin must learn that two plus two equals four—and not five. If Kevin hadn't figured out how to solve this problem before he took the standardized math test, then his teacher—or another teacher the following year—will get another shot at it. Kevin's teachers will have reached remediation conclusions based on their experience, education, and professionalism. This formula for learning recovery is tried and true, so barring the possibility that Kevin's teacher is a lazy bum, it should work for Kevin (and the rest of the kids, too).

Regrettably, Kevin may never learn how to add (and subtract and multiply and divide or anything else in the math arena). No teacher, not even one directly recruited from *Waiting For Superman*, will discover a way to teach him this. And all the hoopla, energy, and paranoia that is emitted from those educator meetings is for nothing. Nothing. *Nothing.* Valuable time and resources have been wasted. No matter what we do to ameliorate the crisis, the next time the Kevins are tested in math, their results will induce our gag reflux. Again.

The solution isn't to blame teachers, torture students, and pour millions of dollars into another black hole; the solution is to acknowledge that these tests *reek*.

And then to act accordingly.

Hurts Teachers

American teachers have given tests to their students ever since the days of *The Little House on the Prairie*. Throughout the years, some teachers have tested too much and others have tested too little. Some teachers have designated their courses' tests as an integral part of their teaching, often utilizing exams as a major focus of their assessment of student achievement; other teachers have used course tests only as a matter of formality. These teachers may not be rigorous enough. Perhaps, they used—to varying degrees of success—other viable methods of assessment. But since the beginning of time—pre–Common Core—the powers that be allowed teachers the latitude to make decisions regarding testing according to what those teachers deemed, in their professional judgment (there's that word *professional* again), in the best interests of the specific children they were working with at the moment. This meant teachers could test a tiny bit, test a lot, or test not at all.

Some teachers used performance projects (plays, skits, interviews, speeches) in lieu of written final exams or midterms. Teachers assign essays, research papers, or art tasks. Teachers also possessed the discretionary power to speak with their students one-on-one, presenting their test questions to them through that personal venue.

Imagine coming into your classroom at lunch to talk to your English teacher: she asks you questions—interview style—about the novel you read or the poems you studied or the class discussions you had. You are offered an opportunity to ask him questions, too: for your own clarification or to lighten up the mood. If your teacher is willing to take the time, he assesses your knowledge of the subject—and then some (what's in your heart and soul, for example).

Yes, this is a monstrous undertaking on the part of the teacher. It requires brilliant planning, courageous effort, and interminable patience on his part. And guess what: teachers willingly go above and beyond the call of duty if they figure they can serve their students, schools, and communities better than others did in the past. More teachers fit into this mold than much of the public recognizes.

Unfortunately, state- and federally sponsored exams fall beyond the control of any teacher to make a professional judgment. Government forces teachers to assess by using bubble sheets or computer templates (the wave of the future: computer testing).

Excessive, mostly pointless, testing in the public schools hurts teachers.

1. Teachers must take the time to administer the tests.

Testing takes up a tremendous amount of time. Teachers would be better off doing other things. And so would their students.

2. Tests devour classroom instructional opportunities.

Of course, students are hurt here, too—primarily students—but teachers have passions, and one of those passions is to *teach*.

3. Tests require teachers to align their curriculum with what other teachers of the same subject are doing.

Aligning subject matter curriculum is not necessarily a good thing for students or teachers, and the *imposition* of this philosophy is bad for teachers.

4. Tests stress out teachers.

This stress causes physical and mental maladies that hamper teachers in both their personal and professional lives.

5. Tests challenge teachers' professionalism.

Excessive standardized tests basically say to teachers (and the others who are paying attention to what's going on these days in the public schools), "*We do not trust you to depart your wisdom, teach the curriculum, and to assess your students; therefore,* we *are going to test your students up the butt in order to confirm our suspicions: you are incompetent, we plan to pay you less money, and our children are dumb, mainly because of you.*"

6. Test scores are used to justify paying teachers more, or less, money.

Some states have established criteria in order to determine the best teachers. And they pay the "best teachers" more money, based on their students' scores on standardized tests. This practice has been ineffective.[9] But in a ranking of about ten criteria, test results are near the bottom when it comes to determining overall teaching effectiveness; and in some subjects, such as art and physical education, no tests can be given to assess degrees of achievement.[10]

7. Testing contributes to teachers looking bad

The public thinks teachers construct the tests (*and when the tests reek, it's the teacher's fault*).

Students think the teachers like giving these tests (*which they absolutely do not*).

Leaders in government and *education* think that tests should determine teachers' employment status, salary, and bonus pay *(which is just another way to broadcast how short-sighted these people are about what constitutes teacher competency)*.

Everybody thinks students' scores on tests are an indication of how well their teachers taught them (*which it could be, but isn't always; and teachers have no direct control over how their own students perform on tests they, the teachers, are coerced into promoting*).

A lot of people think high, or low, test scores in a school are *the* major determinant of how good a school is, or how bad it is; and if it's bad, there must be lots of bad teachers at that school (*completely decimating the reputation of the vast majority of teachers at that school who are actually pretty good*).

Many people think teachers whose students do particularly well on exams must have cheated or encouraged their students to cheat; teachers sometimes are accused—at least, informally—of cheating (*and an accusation of cheating is worse for a teacher's reputation than an accusation of incompetence, but not quite as bad as an accusation of being a Republican*).

Students think testing really stinks, and they also think it's their teachers' fault they have to take so many tests (*which, of course, is a testament that students are still children and are uninformed, misled, and ignorant of the truth: teachers hate testing as much as their students do*).

Overall, almost everyone thinks that tests, in the modern climate, reflect the state of education, and bad test results signify bad schools; bad schools, of course, come as the result of bad teachers (*and everything else wrong with America, as a result, is blamed on teachers, including global warming*).

Denise Jenkins, a veteran teacher in Kansas City, quipped, "I lug around the baggage of being the cause of the demise of modern American education, without the benefit of knowing that when education gets better—it has to get better—anyone will think it's because of me or any other teacher in the United States."[11]

8. Tests stifle a teacher's creativity

If tests are *everything*, which they *are*, if tests largely determine the employment status of teachers, which they *do*, if tests drain the budget of most school districts in ways they have never done before, which happens, the sensible thing for any teacher is to find out what is covered on those tests and then teach directly to them; that is, all material covered in the classroom is geared toward answering specific test questions.

Teaching to the test can be accomplished through rote memorization practices, redundant drills, and even, um, *cheating*. There are numerous methods for teachers to use in order to cheat the system and, ultimately, the kids they are supposed to be serving. Teachers aligning their instruction directly to the test and finding devious, underhanded ways to slip their students the correct answers *has* to be a concern for those who care about the integrity of American education.

Mandates for Discomfort

School used to be kind of fun. Kids looked forward to recess and lunch. They happily awaited the occasional creative activity right in their very own classrooms! Even high school kids occasionally played around a tad; they may have even laughed once or twice during the course of a school day. But an abundance of tests has changed much of that. Teachers now feel a need to act tough, be firm, and toe the mark—consistently.

The mood of our schools has shifted from being a somewhat pleasant experience to rivaling China and South Korea for infanticide. It's sickening: yes, children literally get sick of school. They become ill.[12] The negatives of excessive testing exacerbate the other reasons children can't tolerate going to school.

DUBIOUS MOTIVES

The various powers that be used to administer exams to schoolchildren for the purpose of evaluating how much those children had learned in specific courses. The students would be given a grade, one that, theoretically, accurately represented their achievement in those courses. Sure, there was the occasional intrusion by state or local governments. They wished to have a couple of fingers in the pudding. Even the federal government sometimes became involved in testing. Overall, though, these intrusions didn't occur often. Nowadays, tests occupy an enormous portion of the education landscape.

Ironically, that which "they" thought would make things better actually made things worse; and a big reason for this is that tests, many of them gratuitous, are too often dumped on students and teachers for the wrong reasons.

Testing for Subject Competence

On the surface, this reason for giving a test appears to be valid; however, if anyone thinks *teachers* who have designed and taught their courses should be the ones who actually control the content and level these exams, then mass testing by hired, outside bureaucrats is ridiculous and wasteful.

Testing for Standards Competence

Unless teachers *teach to the test*—the actual standardized test—assessing standards competence is inefficient and inaccurate. The idea of producing a cute little set of standards all teachers in every subject area can agree upon is sweet. But it's foolhardy. Teachers often scratch their heads in bewilderment when they ponder the identity of those who decide for *everybody* else what *all* children are supposed to learn in each and every grade level, about the same time, and across America (and now, with IB, around the world). *Who are these people?* Who anointed them?

Even veteran teachers, many of whom have been bestowed with the highest honors, don't know who comes up with these things! For example, consider this language arts standard in California: *Students will distinguish the differences between hyperbole and simile and cite a passage of literature to substantiate their claim.*[13]

Testing for Advanced Placement Courses

Until 1980, there was no such thing as an advanced placement class. While students were in high school, they could take *honors* courses, but anyone could get into one of those. All that was required of students who wanted to study in an honors English course was a desire for extra tutelage in literature and writing. This meant that the teachers would deluge students with infinitely more work than they would have received in a regular English class.

In those days, students in honors courses did not earn an extra grade point, so the true impetus for striving to become thoroughly inundated in the study of English was a *desire* to do so. Sometimes students saw honors courses as an academic status symbol, but more often, parents believed their children in honors classes to be the safeguards of their worldwide parenting reputation.

Eliminate the extra grade point. Assign students to AP classes, with deference to their previous English teacher's recommendations and/or a sample of their writing. Even a summer project for AP candidates might weed out the serious from the silly. But another asinine, nonconclusive exam: Why?

Sometimes educators don't think things through. Testing for getting permission to take AP courses is one of those times.

Perhaps, there is little that public educators can do about the colleges and universities mandating a test in order to offer certain waivers to students who demonstrate proficiency in various subjects; however, simply to jump on the testing bandwagon doesn't seem academic or free-spirited, especially for a university.

Colleges and universities used to test incoming students *away* from certain courses; this was how lots of people avoided having to take low-level English courses during their freshman year. But those tests were done during the early summer and free from the interferences and roadblocks that normally gunk up high schools.

Testing for Graduation Proficiency

What can be said about an exam that is supposed to test students for what they should know by the time they have graduated from high school—hence, called an *exit exam*—but is given to students *during their sophomore year* of high school![14] 'Nuff said about this, except to point out that it is teachers who, unfortunately, wind up taking the blame for this statehouse ludicrousness.

Overall, it is teachers who take the blame for almost everything testing-wise, in a slightly bent form of the old credo: *If you don't like the message, blame the messenger.* Here, it is, *if you don't like the testing policy, blame the poor sucker who is forced to administer it.*

Today's various systems and modalities of testing leave a lot to be desired.

Teachers' advocate, W. James Popham, observed, "Standardized achievement tests should not be used to judge the quality of education. . . . Any inference about education quality made on the basis of students' standardized achievement test performance is apt to be invalid."[15]

The system that propagates these inadequacies undermines the successes of American teachers: in the eyes of the public, in the esteem of other educators, and in the view of the students to whom most teachers are firmly committed.

NOTES

1. This is blatantly untrue. But in a subjective realm, it could be effectively argued in a court of law.

2. These are her actual words, edited, but the essence of what she says is captured. Unfortunately.

3. Bridget Wassermann, "The Trial of a Thousand Ideas," *The Waverly Symposium*, March–June 2015, 4–5.

4. "Children Should Play in the Dirt . . . " *Mirror*, May 2016, http://www.mirror.co.uk/news/world-news/children-should-play-dirt-stop-7984328.

5. Your humble author, after his first child was born, moved from a subpar neighborhood into a par neighborhood. The home values soared. But people still called me, begging to buy my house. Why? The elementary school down the street had an Academic Performance Index (API) score of around 850. Ironically, the school wasn't that great: few activity programs, low teacher pay, and deteriorating classrooms. But one thing was for certain: those little kids really knew how to take state-mandated tests!

6. The Cubs may have won by the time you read this. It is unlikely, but they do have a better team now. Most baseball fans think the Cubs will blow it.

7. Stephanie Lu, "So Why Do So Many Japanese Children Kill Themselves?" *Newsweek*, November 8, 2015, 1.

8. From a while ago, but nothing has changed in this realm, which is a big reason why we have this problem.

9. Steven Glazerman and Allison Seifullah, "An Evaluation of the Teacher Advancement Program (TAP) in Chicago: Year Two Impact Report," Mathematical Policy Research, May 17, 2010, http://www.mathematica-mpr.com/publications/pdfs/education/tap_yr2_rpt.pdf. See more at: http://parentsacrossamerica.org/performancepay/#sthash.QAfwqNk7.dpuf.

10. Sean P. Corcoran, "Can Teachers Be Evaluated by Their Students' Test Scores? Should They Be?" Annenberg Institute for School Reform, 2010. www.annenberginstitute.org/pdf/valueAddedReport.pdf. See more at: http://parentsacrossamerica.org/performancepay/#sthash.QAfwqNk7.dpuf.

11. The irony is that on anyone's competency scale, Denise is one of the best teachers around (or was, because Denise recently hung up her chalkboard and replaced it with a travel guide).

12. Gilda Leiberman, clinical psychologist, interview, May 5, 2016.
13. Stephen Wall, "Bill Calls for Halting High School Exit Exam," *Senate Newsletter*, July 5, 2015, http://sd31.senate.ca.gov/news/2015-07-05-bill-calls-halting-high-school-exit-exam.
14. Some states, including California in 2015, abandoned administering high school exit exams.
15. W. James Popham, "A Friend in Need," Testing and Assessment Forum, Whittier College, 1991.

Chapter Six

Good Teachers, Bad Advocates

It is time to be totally up-front.

Which, in real-world terms, means it is time to level with one another.

Which, in language that everybody can understand, means it is time to hear the truth. Your thoughts about teachers are documented up the gazinky (and some people have very large gazinkies).

So it is time that someone—namely this author, because it is this book you are reading—tells you the absolute, unadulterated, unrestrained (oftentimes shocking) truth about America's teachers. It ain't gonna be pretty at times, but right now the education establishment isn't pretty, either. What's happening to children isn't pretty, either. And the aspersions, innuendos, and lies about America's teachers are not pretty, either. By casting the die of veracity upon the land, the truths may be sorted from the lies, and the heart of the matter emerges, waiting to be seen for what it is: *where our teachers have mucked it up*.

1. America's teachers have been sheep to their union leaders.

Not saying that unions aren't helpful; in fact, during the past three years, teachers in the United States have been the recipients of salary and benefit increases of nearly 7 percent (on average).[1]

There has been a tug of war among the various public employees unions. There is only so much money to go around; everyone wants his negotiating reps to grab for the biggest piece of the pie. Jim Riches of the New York City Fire Department observed, "Education is valuable, absolutely yes. You cannot do without it. But take away too many firefighters and police, and you'll have more fires where people get killed. . . . Crime will go up."[2]

But therein also lies a dilemma: unions have been good for teachers (and most other public employees), in the sense that unions bring teachers *stuff*.

But in their earnest attempts to help teachers in a myriad of ways, these unions have also accumulated a whole host of criticisms, most of them deserved.

- *Unions go to bat for bad teachers.*
- *Unions coerce teachers to join them (or alternative programs for which unions, despite a teacher's philosophical objections, extract money from their paychecks).*
- *Unions support left-wing political candidates and causes.*
- *Unions' egalitarian policies, such as regularly moving teachers from school to school, diminish excellence in education.*
- *Unions have undue influence on officeholders.*
- *Unions mandate absurd, counterproductive, expensive policies—all in the name of the union trademark.*

Rather than defending these flaws, educators should admit to them. They're true. Unions have been good, mainly for higher salaries, better working conditions (though not all the time: sometimes worse working conditions), and superior fringe benefits.

Just how do these factors improve the lot of children? One could argue that when a teacher is happy, her students are happy. But a direct correlation on this touchy-feely concept has never been made, hypothesized without viable evidence. Yet educators argue it all the time, especially teachers; they argue it a lot: *if I'm feeling happier, my students will be happier.*

Teachers are flawed, and their unions don't help their image: they tarnish it. Teachers' unions project negative images to the rest of society, outside education.[3]

2. *America's teachers complain too much.*

And who wants to hear it?

"*I may get the summers off, but I don't get paid for those days I don't work!*"

Seriously? You don't get paid for the days you *don't* work? Wow. Even Tom Joad, in *The Grapes of Wrath*, spoke of a man's worth being measured in the fairness of a hard day's work for a fair day's pay. Do you think Tom would have been happy with a fair day's pay for a hard day's work? Did he ever gripe about not being paid for the days he *didn't* work? Just wondering.[4]

"*I have extra duties outside the classroom!*"

You teach inside your classroom until 2:00 or 3:00 P.M. Then you must take tickets at the afternoon football game or, worse, come back later in the evening once or twice a month to chaperone a dance. Perhaps, you have to coach the fourth-graders' academic challenge group two times a week. And here comes the topper. . . . You volunteer your lunchtime once a week in order to tutor students who are having difficulties in their studies!

All that: ticket taker or dance chaperone or academic coach or tutor . . . whew! You are not paid for those hours you work beyond your classroom! That's a tough pill to swallow.

"Nobody understands what I go through!"

You may be right about that one. But nobody gives a hoot about your plight in the classroom. They figure it goes with the territory. If you're a teacher, you're supposed to be miserable. If you've embarked upon a career in education, you are occasionally going to be looked upon askance and with disdain.

Young people who go into education with an eye toward winning a popularity contest are projected to leave the profession years ahead of those who don't have that expectation. Teachers quickly realize—and must accept—teaching as a rugged, tough, and challenging profession. Either they get over themselves, or they succumb to the pressures of the job they have chosen.

"I am overworked!"

Really? Reread the chapter about the coal miners.

That concept is subjective, anyway. And it's relative. In this day and age, what does *overworked* mean? This author's teenage son complains of being overworked if he is told to make his bed *and* pick up the trash from his bedroom floor—all in the same morning! Garage mechanics who put in eleven hours six days a week and receive maybe forty-five minutes for lunch . . . that means overworked, too.

Everybody in America is overworked. Unless they are underworked. And that is just as bad—probably a lot worse.

"I can do so much more with my life."

Okay, here comes one of the most serious concepts in this book: look again at this teacher's complaint. And then look *again*. Please. If you have made that complaint more than once, you should not have gone into teaching in the first place.

You think you could have done so much more with your life: so much more than guiding and directing young people to happy, fulfilling lives, to opening up doors for them that would have never been opened, to saving lives—literally—saving lives that would have otherwise been wasted.

You can do so much more with *your* life?

Maybe.

Maybe not.

Sign your resignation letter tonight—before you do any more damage.

"It's so hard not being around adults all day!"

Some people never grow up, particularly men: some men are fourteen when they are chronologically forty-four. That's a tough fact of life. Adults are dwindling in numbers. Sometimes teachers are around more adults at their schools than they are when they step out into the real world ... or when they go home to their spouses.

But come on! Teachers should have known—guess what?—they are destined to work mostly with children during their hours on the job! Teachers who realize there are children around them only *after* they have been teaching for a while are not exactly the brightest bulbs. *Hey, man! What? I gotta hang around kids all day?*

There are numerous complaints from teachers that others hear, over and over again. This, then, constitutes the second indictment of teachers, a concession to one of their inadequacies: *teachers complain a lot.*

3. Teachers are horrible advocates for themselves.

The above statement is not a reference to teachers' *unions* not being good advocates. The unions are terrific advocates ... for the unions. As for unions being effective advocates for individual teachers, that may be an entirely different story. But teachers, the rank and file, the individual human beings that comprise the teaching profession—Uncle Carl and Cousin Jose, neighbor Billy and stranger Willie—*these* teachers don't do much to advocate for their profession.

Complaining incessantly about your lot in life because you became a teacher or decrying young people for being stupid and not knowing the information *that you were supposed to have taught them* is not first-rate public relations, not positive representation for you as a teacher and, by transfer, for all other teachers across the land.

Mr. Calderon, the principal of Bolton Way Middle School, has congregated fifty-eight teachers and twelve subordinate staff members in the multipurpose room at his school for what he has termed an *emergency meeting*. Wearing a well-manicured, immaculate suit and tie, he stands before this group of somewhat uneasy adults, allowing nothing to obscure him—even partially—from his audience. Mr. Calderon is a well-built, youngish forty-year-old, who stands over six feet tall. Normally, his chiseled, shaven face is set in a relaxed posture. Today, he appears tense, his jaw squarely set, his eyes narrowed.

Mr. Calderon spends thirty minutes informing his staff of a communication he received from the district superintendent. He uses PowerPoint technology in a darkened room. Evidently, a group of angry homeowners in the community spoke before the school board; they shared their concern over decreasing home values in the neighborhood. They blamed that depreciation on the bad reputation of the local middle school, Mr. Calderon's school. The homeowners argued that there was a direct correlation between the state's standardized test scores and *what others deemed to be the quality of a school*. High scores, equals quality schools. Low scores, equals ineffectual schools.

Mr. Calderon winds down his angry tirade with the following comments: "You and I know, as educators, that none of this is true. We know a test score alone does not reflect how good or bad a school is. We know that a single snapshot of a high school, as shown in an even smaller snapshot in the form of a state sponsored test, does not tell us anything substantive about a school's worth. But it doesn't matter. We have to do better. *You have to do better*. You teachers are inside the classroom with your students, day in and day out. You constantly tell anyone who will listen this truth—that you are the ones in the trenches. The rest of us are tantamount to standing on the sidelines. All right, prove it. If you are the ones in the trenches with the kids, then for God's sake, *save somebody*!"

Those teachers of whom Mr. Calderon speaks, the ones who have been held captive by this man for over thirty minutes, sit there, motionless: some display shock on their faces; others appear perfectly bland, as though they have absorbed nothing. Others barely stir, only to peek at their cell phones.

These hard-working men and women, some of whom have been teaching at the same school for thirty to forty years, have been dumped on by a young neophyte who never set foot inside a classroom as a teacher. But he, like many others in education, feel the pangs of pressure from abroad, from others who may have been nameless and faceless and ignorant and wrong—but, nevertheless, carried clout. Where this clout came from, and just exactly how it had gotten to the point it had, is not clear.

Stagnation. Humiliation.

They go hand in hand. The faculty and staff at Mr. Calderon's school is paralyzed by humiliation. And they won't respond productively, either. They probably will regress. Their fate as a school has been sealed. Even worse for the teachers, another nail has been hammered into their career coffins.

How could these teachers just sit there while Mr. Calderon went on and on? How could they not have recoiled in anger or, at least, offered remarks that would have refuted their principal's condemnation, or the orders that got Mr. Calderon reluctantly in front of his faculty in the first place?

Cowards?

Exhaustion?

Resignation?

Indifference?

All—or some—of these?

They just sat there.

Here is what *should have happened*, the scenario that would have proven one of the theses of this book completely wrong and, ultimately, would have ridden along as a savior, at least for this group of educators. The last words of Mr. Calderon's address in front of his faculty were: "If the staff at this school spent but a fraction of the time that they spent complaining in pursuit of lofty goals and producing substantive programs to become better teachers, then all of our students would not only graduate with honors, they would all be Harvard bound!"

Two teachers, middle-aged men who had been at the school for over ten years, rose in the back of the room. They turned their backs to their principal and silently marched out of the auditorium. Another teacher, a robust-looking woman in her forties, without rising, said from her seat. "What do you know about lofty goals and substantive programs, Mr. Calderon? For the five years you have been here, we have had neither!"

Before the principal could respond, an older male teacher said, "We didn't have them before he got here, either."

"And why not?" asked a young man from the front. He had risen from the first row and half turned to the rest of the group. "We didn't have them, because we have been so busy trying to keep up with the fast pace of things, and with all the changes."

"Yeah," said the heavyset woman, "like the changing technology. You've delivered projectors to my classroom that look like weapons from *Star Wars*."

Another teacher, deliberate and contemplative, said, "Either we settle right now on what we need to do for these kids, or there will be hell to pay at the district office. And I, for one, will see to it that some administrators' heads roll. Every time we fail around here, we teachers get blamed. That's wrong. It's not our fault, not to the extent people are saying. Teachers are taking a bad rap for things that have gone wrong, and that's over, starting now!"

A woman in a dark pantsuit stood at her seat. She shook her fist. "I'm tired of this! I'm inviting all of you to march on the school board tomorrow night. Get parents to support us, too, because we are all in this together!"

An aggressive commotion swept the meeting room. The principal pounded the gavel (figuratively speaking, of course, because there was no gavel).

What just transpired here? Something unique, unusual, downright weird has occurred. Teachers stood up for themselves! They shouted bold, daring, and intelligent ideas as they defended themselves from short-sighted, willy-nilly comments spewed out by their authority figures, comments that would serve no end, except to make the teachers feel bad about themselves and the current state of education.

Perhaps, if such expressions of derision improved the schools, they would serve a greater good. But that is not the case. The constant cajoling by highly educated individuals does nothing productive. Instead, the opposite occurs. Belittling people when they are down produces a cowering clientele, not a stronger one. The impetus to get better disintegrates. The dust left behind sifts through the fingers of those who stand in bewilderment: *You have failed us. You have frustrated us. And it is clearly the fault of educators.*

Teachers rarely stand up for themselves. They haven't a forum to do so.

School board meetings are usually robotic assemblies that play to a handful of constituents in mostly empty rooms. Besides, when it comes to being heard, teachers who attend school board meetings sit on the lower rungs of the importance ladder.

Newspapers and other publications used to have some clout when it came to swaying public opinion; they no longer do. Who reads these things anymore?

Strikes and other work stoppages were once tools of protest, taking on critics of teachers and those scoundrels who would diminish teachers' salaries or worsen their working conditions. Teacher strikes are now seen as left-wing, extremist acts by fringe elements that have no regard for how hard other people work, especially those in the private sector. Strikes have hardly been a solid form of self-expression for America's teachers.

Public gatherings used to be places where people talked about the events of the day: parties, political rallies, sporting events, and Eminem concerts. Teachers had a forum at these places; they were often the brunt of a joke or the object of ridicule. Most people had the decency to allow teachers to defend themselves.

Public gatherings today are useless. People don't stray to these types of issues. They don't discuss education. And they spend an inordinate amount of time checking for terrorists and fondling their cellphones.

Social media has been a rat hole for complaints, and in recent years, it has been the dumping ground for more rhetorical garbage than it can handle. Hardly anybody pays serious attention to what is said on social media; and if they do, most of it becomes garbled into a mesh of verbal diarrhea. If a teacher presents her case on a social media site, Twitter, Facebook, and the like, hardly anyone, unless she looks like Megyn Kelly, focuses on what she says. If she is lucky enough to capture someone else's attention, she is usually the object of scorn and ridicule by dozens—sometimes hundreds—of other tweeters and posters.

Those who think they are making their case for teachers on social media are fooling themselves and, in the process, look pathetic.

What's grim about this situation is the banal attitude of teachers. But it's understandable. Once you have been the victim of a continuous kicking and mauling, you don't feel much like walking into the dark alley for another round of abuse.

Why complain to an uninterested, at best, and unsympathetic, at worst, electorate about how you feel so maligned and unappreciated? No one cares. You look like a spoiled schoolgirl. You appear ungrateful and unfeeling. You, who have your summers and vacations off; you, who have full medical and dental benefits; you, who have safe and attractive retirement programs listed in your name—why should anyone else listen to your piddling little complaints about your strife at work?

Bad economies are terrible for teachers. They limit jobs, cut programs, and piss off the public. Teachers have the challenge of actually being hired for a stable job they can go to every day, being granted money for supplies in their classrooms, and being gazed upon by the public as pillars of altruism when it comes to kids. Complaining about your lot accomplishes none of these things.

Teachers are bad advocates for themselves. This may not be a concern for the general public, but knowledge of this weakness may help others to adjust their feelings about the teaching profession. At any rate, move on to another gripe about teachers.

4. Teachers can't do anything else, so they teach.

Most teachers count their lucky stars that they don't have to get real jobs. They wouldn't know what a real job looked like, even if one came right up and whacked them with a dry-erase marker. Plumbers, pipe fitters, painters, auto mechanics—you want to hear more real jobs?—machinists, supermarket clerks, coal miners . . . these are *real* jobs.

When English teacher Mr. Bernstein's wife tells him they have a leaky pipe under the sink, he calmly nods, fetches the wrench . . . hands it to her, and holds her feet steady while her face and body are thrust into the darkness of the sink's cabinet, as she fixes the leaky pipe. Mr. Bernstein doesn't know a wrench from a hammer. But he can explain the difference between a compound and complex sentence to seventh graders who are still picking their noses and eating their discoveries. But that's not a real job. Fixing leaks: that *is* a real job.

There is some truth to teachers having a limited amount of professional or vocational expertise outside the classroom. But so what? The majority of America's teachers did not back into their professions. They set goals long ago, planned how they were going to meet those goals, and thousands of dollars and several years later, they arrived . . . only to be accused of not knowing how to do anything else—so what the heck!

Woody Allen, in his masterpiece *Annie Hall*, utters the famous line, "Those who can't do, teach. And those who can't teach, teach physical education."[5]

Teachers shouldn't be angry with that. They should *laugh*—even physical education teachers.

People often go from professions in which they actually *do* things, into teaching; for example, a woman who does the books for a large financial firm gets sick of doing the books and decides she wants to teach math or economics to children. She works for a few years on acquiring teaching credentials, and then becomes a high school math instructor. This rather weird individual could make twice as much money as an accountant or a bookkeeper, but her heart (certainly not her brain) sent her on a merry journey into public education.

Every year thousands of men and women make the same journey. Countless teachers look back at their former jobs and breathe a sigh of relief that they became teachers. Of course, some of those teachers curse the day they thought the grass was greener on the other side and made the switch into education.

People who, for example, own their own tutoring businesses are not used to bubble-gum chewing, screeching teenagers who were up all night playing video games or watching reruns of *The Walking Dead.* Now they are forced to deal with real-life teenagers, those kids who are chaperoned at the tutoring center by parents who come from cultures in which they eat their kids alive if they don't receive straight-As in school.

Teachers are capable of doing others things. Multitalented teachers are, in fact, a good fit *because* of their many talents: musically inclined teachers organize concerts; thespian teachers direct plays; athletic teachers coach sports. Various industries offer up their teachers on a silver platter, and from all walks of life: business, cinema, finance, public service, politics, mechanics, and . . . you get the point.

Teachers and real life cross over. Men and women do not teach because they are incompetent at anything else. They do not teach because their lives are otherwise irrelevant. (This is not to say that sometimes these things are true.) They teach because they *want* to. Some teachers have goals their entire lives that are centered around their eventual positions in education. To relegate these people to a secondary status in society because they are teaching instead of doing, is to cavalierly dismiss the fact that many *once did*. Or they *could do*, if they wanted.

5. America's teachers attract people with a Napoleon Complex.

Napoleon Complex has to do with a short man who feels strongly about wielding a lot of power in order to make up for his deficiency in the height department. Unless most of these teachers with a Napoleon Complex are, indeed, vertically challenged, this concept does not apply to them; at least, not exactly.

What *does* apply to these teachers is, *perhaps*, the notion that men and women who feel feeble or powerless in most facets of their lives try to compensate for their inadequacies by reigning with authority wherever they can, in a career that offers them the opportunity to do so. Power over children, influencing kids, molding young people is the aphrodisiac they have been looking for.

Nobody is running around saying stuff like, "All teachers want is power. They want to boss people around. They have little, lousy lives, and the charge they get from being a teacher makes up for that."

Yawn.

Okay, there are certain admissions due here: teachers are weird, for one. They are a special lot, and they have their idiosyncrasies like anybody else. But—and here is the big *but*—their "power fetish" is merely their affection for teaching young people: about life, history, math, science, civics, and so on. It's not power for the sake of power. It's not an impish, evil craving to boss children around or affect the dynamics of families. Some people are, simply, born to teach. They are the good ones. They are the special—and, perhaps, the few.

Everyone wants to change the world. Some wish to make small changes that create a better situation for *them*; others desire to make changes that will bolster society; at least, according to their prejudices and specifications. Still others want to affect the world in a huge way: they yearn to make discoveries, medical and technological and scientific, that would alter the course of civilization.

Professor Cramer, of Whittier College, contended, "There are two types of individuals who call themselves *people persons:* those who are driven by authentic desires to see others succeed. For them, knowledge of the successes of others is enough to satisfy, to bring them joy. And those who are driven by their self-absorbed goals to make themselves look good, to bring attention to their own achievements, which are now measured by the resulting successes of those they helped."

For some teachers, their students' achievements are not inherently enough; only their connection as a teacher brings them satisfaction. These teachers may have the Napoleon Complex (or a teacher's version of it) or other psychological challenges that may have stayed with them since childhood. But when kids learn, when they enjoy school, when they score high, however their achievement is measured, *everybody* wins: teachers, students, the education establishment, and society.

By and large, even when factoring in the most pernicious criticisms of teachers, America's educators do a darn good job of holding down the fort while their students' parents are away, scavenging for food.

NOTES

1. Extrapolated—and states differ. California has given several salary and benefit increases to teachers in the past four years. In Texas, teacher salaries went up an average of around 3 percent in 2015.

2. Alan Farnham, "Cops vs Teachers: Who's Worth More in Tight Times?" ABC News, February 28, 2011, http://abcnews.go.com/Business/firemen-cops-versus-teachers-nurses-state-budget-crises/story?id=13003968.

3. Mercedes White, "Support for Teachers Unions at an All-Time Low," *Deseret News*, June 13, 2012, http://www.deseretnews.com/article/865557379/Support-for-teachers-unions-at-an-all-time-low.html?pg=all.

4. One of the biggest complaints about teachers I receive from laypeople: "Why do teachers gripe so much about not getting paid for days they don't work?" Perhaps, teachers should stop this. It makes us look bad. Really bad.

5. *Annie Hall*, Rollins-Joffe Productions, 1977: starring Woody Allen and Diane Keaton. This Best Picture, Academy Award–winning film was chock-full of memorable one-liners, and this comment about teachers is among the most memorable—and funniest.

Chapter Seven

Feeding the Hand That Bites You

The coal miners were your guiding light ... to the career you did *not* want to gravitate to. Teachers were your inspiration, establishing an image in your mind for what you *did* wish to become. And then you did. You spent much of your life teaching young people. You departed your knowledge, your wisdom. You fought off those who would try to punch holes in your quest: administrators, parents, government, and even some of the students you taught.

Nothing was ever perfect, absolutely the way you wanted it to be or intended it to be. But it was close enough. Teaching all these years made you feel special; you *were* special. You made a name for yourself. You established your mark and then succeeded in making it.

No one could ever take that away from you.

Or could he?

Potter Restock said, "Veteran teachers have a vested interest in maintaining the integrity of their successors ... young teachers, the newbies."[1] People tend to remember with clarity what happened to them lately—who affected them *lately*. Older teachers are cherished for their enthusiasm, their wisdom, and their industriousness. Younger teachers are often portrayed as rebellious, angry, insecure. If those three words—rebellious, angry, insecure—signify the teachers of today, the profession will be assuredly remembered for how it is currently branded.[2]

Several educators, some of them retired, and a few veterans still hanging in there, have contributed to this section of the text. Their interest is to help teachers, but it is also to protect their own reputations. The honorableness of the teaching profession—then and now—depends on a visceral willingness of teachers to fix those elements in their lives that have led them down a path to visible consternation among the general public and government leaders.

Tweaking a few aspects of the system—okay, *more* than merely tweaking these things—would go a long way toward rebounding teacher integrity.

In no particular order of importance:

1. Establish uniform qualifications and teacher credentialing standards.
2. Shrink class sizes.
3. Offer merit pay.
4. Undercut the power of teachers unions.
5. Contain student testing.
6. Support teachers, not disruptive students.
7. Dispel myths about improper teacher conduct.
8. Publicize the *facts* about due process—*not* tenure—protections.
9. Reevaluate Common Core and other innovative education programs.
10. Advocate school choice.

Much of what is advocated here is already being done. Many of these ideas have already been implemented. But the people don't know. Politicians don't know. Among those who do know, personal agendas have kept them from caring. The force behind the movement to defend America's teachers has to come from three sources: teachers, parents, and students. Readers of this book, if they are not among those mentioned, can help, too. Teachers want everybody's help, but gains are best made at the grassroots level. They can inspire others to follow suit.

Sometimes the general public does not consider basic, rudimentary concepts concerning changes in our schools—like money, for example. They assume that people can do whatever they want if they are in a position of power. But, of course, they can't. Despite the know-it-all's claim that more money in education would be like throwing thousand dollar bills into a furnace, their symbolism is ludicrous. More money for our schools would sometimes be wasteful; other times, more money could save someone's life. Individual cases are particular; they are different from each other. They demand separate solutions and careful individual analysis.

If the police force were being referenced here, or the fire department, there would be a serious, cooperative quest to reform policies that required reforming, not generalizations about the polices' inadequacies. Not to make changes, to continue to complain and badger, make absolutely no sense.

1. Establish uniform qualifications and teacher credentialing standards.

Some states license teachers after requiring them to student teach under the guidance of a master teacher. Other states do not require student teaching, per se. Some states require teachers to go through tedious amounts of training and research in order to renew their credentials; other states require them to go through a sequential three to five years of licensing, simply upon their application for renewal. Some states offer only single-subject credentials for their perspective teachers; others offer multisubject credentials that allow them to teach any subject. Some states revoke credentials for the teacher's use of profanity in the classroom; in other states, a teacher would have to kill someone in order for him to lose his credentials. Some states do not honor the licenses of teachers who earned them outside their borders; other states honor the credentials teachers earned even in a foreign country!

Everything would be niftier if standards were uniform across the board, and a teacher could move from Los Angeles to New York and work there without any hassle.

2. Shrink class sizes.

Huge numbers of students in a classroom is the most common complaint of teachers in the United States. It is also a familiar whine of American parents. Even some politicians, those with at least a thimble of wisdom about education, have come to grips with the fact that large class sizes make learning harder for kids, and teaching more difficult for teachers.[3]

Class sizes should be kept down. Teachers would look better to their communities because their students would be more successful. Discipline problems would decrease. There would be fewer kids tempting their teachers to pull every strand of hair from their heads. Raging lunatic teachers would dwindle in number. Too many talking, yelling, laughing kids brew a mixture of confusion and anger in adults. And anger ain't good for a teacher's image.

3. Offer merit pay.

Speaking of crazy, it *is* crazy that merit pay has not been tried by every school district in the United States. Educators who are driven to teach and would do their best, even if they did it for free, are scarce. Those who would donate their time and effort out of benevolence and their love of teaching do exist, but there obviously aren't enough of these people.

The majority of teacher-salary structures in U.S. school districts are designed so that the longer a teacher has been in a school district, and the higher her education attainment, the more money she is going to make. Current teacher salaries at the top of the local scale can be from over a hundred thousand dollars a year (New York), to less than sixty thousand dollars a year (Mississippi). Usually, beginning teachers earn about one-half of the highest salary on the scale; this means that in New York, a first-year teacher would make around $55,000 (not bad for straight out of college!), and that same teacher would take home thirty grand in Mississippi (not nearly as nice, but still pretty cool for a kid just out of college).[4]

Here's the rub, though: teachers make a set amount of dough whether they are teachers who walk on water . . . or teachers who stink up the water. It makes no difference.

Administrators should reward teachers who are exceptional, above and beyond their base salaries. The quibbling about who gets to decide what *exceptional* means needs to stop. *And of course, teacher performance (or merit) pay shouldn't be based on student-achievement testing.* (See chapter 5 for a discussion of that dumb idea.) Simple administrative proclamations about who is superb and who is not should cut the mustard. That's enough. Corporate America makes decisions that way, and those who go around bellyaching about it often wind up begging in the street for their next meal.

4. Undercut the power of teachers unions.

One major problem teachers have with their nasty unions is they do not like their dues going for causes they deplore. In the past, the national branch, during their annual conventions, has stood up for seemingly non-educational-affiliated causes like being pro-choice on abortion, bringing an end to the wars in Iraq and Afghanistan, developing an emergency policy on climate change, and Obamacare.[5]

If you are sitting there dazed and confused, wondering what any of these stances has to do with making America's schools better, join the club. A whole heck of a lot of people don't understand the teachers unions' passions for these types of causes and have a hard time reconciling how much money unions spend for their promotions.

Enter the novel concept of not forcing teachers to pay for these campaigns, and the operations of political candidates, who are almost always liberal Democrats. Some teachers have told their colleagues that a teacher voting for a Republican is like a Jew voting for Hitler.

Okay, perhaps that analogy is a bit far-fetched. But it's been made. It's out there.

The biggest gripe is that the unions are protecting, and sometimes promoting, bad teachers, teachers who are harmful to children.[6] A quick fix to that is to abolish the so-called tenure protections and regulate the system with teacher observations, reviews, and second chances. Nothing has to be set in stone; however, in most jobs, if you mess up a bunch of times, if you hurt the company, if you don't get better at what you do, *you are . . . gone*!

Unions are beneficial for raising money for children's causes, offering scholarships, and helping teachers to get salary and benefit increases. Certainly, if an established, competent teacher is being shafted by a gnarly, vindictive administrator, the union should feverishly work to protect that teacher from any biases or unfairness.

Otherwise, the public's perception of teachers is best served when unions stay out of matters that are not relevant to the education of schoolchildren. After all, educating children is the responsibility of America's teachers; they don't need to attach to an organization that does more harm than good when it comes to that important goal. Richard Berman, of the *Orange County Register*, wrote, "The time for change [education reform] is now, and teachers unions are getting in the way."[7]

5. *Contain student testing.*

When testing policies are brought into the realm of rationality, everybody wins. This concept is discussed at length in chapter 5 ("Not a Teacher's Friend"). Teachers win when student testing is *not* utilized for these purposes:

- To affect teacher salary
- To fire or demote teachers
- To determine property values in the community
- To dictate merit pay for teachers
- To evaluate teacher competency
- To punish teachers by assigning certain students to her classes
- To assign students to honors or AP classes

That last one is particularly controversial. Students who have demonstrated enthusiasm, passion, and prior successes in a subject matter should be allowed to take AP or honors classes. Their fleeting, unreliable results on certain tests should not be a determinant.

6. *Support teachers, not disruptive students.*

The New York City Schools considered Miss Rivera to be one of their gems: "A diamond in the rough," they called her. Of Puerto Rican descent, Miss Rivera was born in the American territory and came to New York with her parents in 1991. She was only eight.

Tragically, not long after Miss Rivera's family had arrived in the Empire State, her father was killed at work by a piece of heavy equipment he had been loading onto a truck. Miss Rivera (first name, Annette) now had only her mother to raise her. Dedicated to her daughter, Annette's mother would never bear another child, taking pride that she spent more hours with Annette than at work. And she spent a lot of time at work!

Annette struggled, but by dedicating herself to her studies and working part-time jobs at various fast-food places, she finished college. In 2006, Miss Rivera, as her students would refer to her, landed her first teaching job, high school math.

Replete with children from broken families and high rates of unemployment, West New York, New Jersey, serviced kids the public and politicians routinely considered destined to fail. It was a classic tough neighborhood, making the characters in *West Side Story* appear as though they were from a musical version of *Leave It to Beaver*.[8]

Although she was pretty and had a personality other teachers on campus were envious of, Miss Rivera didn't date or attend social clubs. She dedicated her life to her students. That was no easy feat. These children were rough!

Each and every day that she was in the classroom, Miss Rivera dealt with contentious students who had no business in the public school system. These kids, who were given chance after chance after chance to succeed (yes, to the point of the ridiculous), continued to fail.

Miss Rivera said, "It wasn't their lack of skills that made things so difficult. It wasn't even their terrible attendance rates, sometimes absent from classes for weeks at a time. My biggest problem with those kids was their rudeness. They were self-absorbed; they had no clue what other students' needs were, whether it was for them to participate in class discussions or—how do I put this?—keep their mouths closed for a minute. I could hardly get in a word without being interrupted. I felt bad for the other students, those who actually wanted to learn, who had a desire to better themselves. Their constant chatter, their loud disruptive comments . . . and their frequent use of profanity."

Miss Rivera paused, tears welling in her eyes, "They drove me out of teaching. I always wanted to teach. But how can a woman teach under conditions like that?"

This touted young teacher, unduly challenged and then utterly wasted, who was just beginning to blossom in a field she had sought to be in her entire life . . . lost to the ravages of a New York slum.

Are teachers expected to be disciplinarians? Absolutely. But teachers are not magicians—at least, the vast majority of them. Most teachers, to varying degrees, are forced to deal with behaviors others only shudder while thinking about:

- Incessant talking to other students
- Direct defiance (ask them to do something, and they refuse)
- Perennial tardiness (being late to class or turning in assignments)
- Extreme rudeness to other students in the class
- Crude remarks about other students, directly or indirectly
- Cheating on tests or homework assignments
- Profanity
- Unsolicited physical contact with another student in the classroom
- Theft inside the classroom
- Moving about the room, or leaving the room, without permission

- Frequent obnoxious laughter (and other disagreeable noises)
- Shouting out or answering questions out of turn or without permission
- Direct verbal confrontations

Those are just for *starters*. When it comes to the *real* issues teachers have to contend with, the hardcore stuff stands alone: alcohol, drugs, weapons. Most teachers confront these problems head-on. When they make a mistake, they get admonished. Other than the requisite lollipop in their mailbox on Teacher Appreciation Day, they are rarely commended for going through their daily routines.

These philosophies put teachers ahead of thugs:

1. The teacher is right, until—and *if*—proven wrong.
2. Schools establish clear guidelines regarding suspension and punishment.
3. Teachers have significant input in their school's discipline policies.
4. Administrators and counselors support teachers until convinced otherwise.
5. Students have the option to withdraw from school after the eighth grade.[9]
6. Class sizes don't exceed the *union's* prescriptions.
7. Occasional school-wide assemblies honor extraordinary teachers.
8. Unilaterally, teachers may temporarily suspend students from their classrooms.
9. Teachers may ask to have students transferred or withdrawn from their classes.
10. The burden of proof lies with the student; presumption is with the teacher.

A cursory analysis of these measures suggests concepts that have been abandoned in the public schools. The new policy in L.A. makes it virtually impossible to suspend a kid from school. Disciplining a class of unruly kids is now a laughable goal. The lenses of political correctness have changed the way schools do business.

These recommendations call for specific actions. They are direct (unilaterally, teachers may temporarily suspend students from their classroom) or attitudinal policy changes that ultimately wind up in the teacher's favor (the teacher is right, until—and *if*—proven wrong).

Teacher-friendly policies and attitudes are long past due.

Teachers should not just advocate here: they should *implore*. They care about kids, for sure. They care about parents. Yup. They have to. They should. They care about society. The net result of developing good laws, policies, and programs is that American society benefits. Society *wins*. The thing to remember, though, is that feeding teachers' appetites for success works in cahoots with everything else talked about in this text. Teachers win; everybody else wins, too.

7. Dispel myths about improper teacher conduct.

American media do not intentionally vilify teachers. To the extent that the stories surrounding child abuse and molestations by teachers are sensationalized, the public can't help but taste bile when hearing or reading about the occasional evil teacher. There is no movement—not a *known* one—to dispel myths and untruths about teachers in this sensitive arena. The images of teachers the media portray malign teachers who have nothing to do with those who should be punished for their unpardonable abuse of children.

8. Publicize the facts about due process—not tenure—protections.

A few reminders about teacher tenure: that many states have reformed or abolished it entirely; that an enormous number of educators have objections to the tenure laws; and that "tenure," as many believe it to be, does not exist. Due process is a procedure that is followed in the American legal system and in most places where people are employed in the United States.

If laypeople decide to be disgruntled about due-process protections, they should remember that teachers unions, undergoing fire from all directions, are blamed for protecting bad teachers. Go ahead and blame almost everything bad about teachers on the unions. That sweeping generality is not entirely valid, but it's close enough for people to see the differences between hardworking, honest, passionate individual teachers—and the monolith that came to represent them.

9. Reevaluate Common Core and other innovative education programs.

This type of thing is done all the time, but public relations is rarely considered when adopting, or trashing, an education reform or new policy. What typically happens—not the fault of the hardworking putz who works wonders with his fourth graders—is that programs come and go, often for no rhyme or reason. Some outsiders believe that teachers have carefully calculated the value of a new program and have, after weighing all the pro and con arguments, streamlined the reform into a neat little package that makes everything that wasn't nice—nice. But it doesn't work that way. Not typically.

Programs *come* when a textbook company markets its latest offering to the various school districts through conferences that originally had nothing to do with that offering. But the textbook is novel and interesting—and piques a lot of interest.

Programs *come* when a single teacher, sometimes with a cohort, writes a book or dreams up a new slant to an old concept and works up a presentation for her own school, her school district's in-services, or for a statewide or national educators' conference.

Programs *come* when wild-eyed educators attend conferences and feast off a special concept or idea they have heard there, trim it to meet their own needs, and then find ways of commercializing it with a textbook company.

Programs *come* when certain influential members of the media pick up on ideas that have been brewing in local school districts. One thing that can be counted on about most media: the more sensational the idea, the more press it will receive. More than one teacher has become famous this way. The mighty press—or website link—never seems to fail.

Programs *come* when educators at conferences are divided into committees and asked to address various problems in the system. Rarely does this occur, but occasionally an idea jolts the senses of others, and attendees at the conference go home with a gleam in their eyes. They can't wait to share their ideas. They can't wait to market what they already began to circulate at the conference as the "Best Thing Since Swiss Cheese"—or whatever.[10]

Programs *go* when administrators at school districts change, and the new superintendent or curriculum director has new and better ideas to throw out there. These new ideas become his own, and current ones get dumped.

Programs *go* when there is sweeping state reform. These reforms hardly ever *trickle* down to local districts; they usually have the weight of a sledgehammer.[11]

Programs *go* when the public raises Holy Hell about them. Enough of the public scoffed at Second to None and No Child Left Behind (NCLB), innovative ideas at one time, to change or entirely abolish those programs.

Programs *go* when they become incorporated into other programs. When new or bigger movements swallow up older, dying movements, educators often shrug and move on, as though the most recent program to succumb never existed in the first place. This is a sweet way of getting rid of something they can't stand anymore.

Programs *go* when federal mandates supersede those programs. No Child Left Behind required states to alter their (at the time, 1998) relatively new state standards reforms. Many states were already incorporating more uniform curriculum and methodologies into their school districts—even funding those reforms.

All through the 1990s, school restructuring was huge. But guess what: when No Child Left behind reared its ill-fated head, along with other laws and guidelines, replete with federal mandates that had to be followed in order to receive funding, the states threw their hands up and complained about wasting their efforts for years. Later, it became abundantly clear that the federal government meant business about its NCLB legislation: that the federal government intended to throw some big bucks at the states, especially for special education programs.

Presto! The education establishment went gaga for No Child Left Behind. The greenback was mightier than the sword, or whatever.

Programs *go* when they, simply, get old. Old people go, too . . . when they get old. It's the natural process, the way of things. You start out young and fresh and vibrant and new, and then you get old and die. That sort of thing also happens to cars. Why should education be any different?

Programs *go* when politicians paint those programs as more despicable than the Boston bombers. In the most recent presidential primary-election cycle, almost every one of the two or three thousand Republicans running for president used rhetoric to describe Common Core as evil as the Nazis. This made an impact. Take a gander at what happened to Jeb Bush, the lone Republican who supported Common Core, as he stammered, hedged, fizzled . . . and died not too deep into the presidential-primary process. Donald Trump also may have had something to do with that stammer, hedge, and fizzle.

10. Advocate school choice.

Teachers don't like school choice advocates very much; that's because when schools are in competition with each other, the crappiest schools won't attract students, and the teachers in those lousy schools may get canned. There are numerous ways of getting around that scenario; it's not a given that teachers will be fired. In the long run, over the passage of (a lot of) time, school choice policies may work beautifully. The free enterprise system works well when there is only a modicum of interference; the interference is in places where the weakest and the most vulnerable are protected by (some) government regulations.

Competition breeds a system that ultimately turns out both winners and losers. Educators, for the most part, already work hard. The difficulty of stepping it up in order to attract clientele to a specific school daunts some teachers.[12]

If only we could cavalierly dismiss the complexities of the school-choice debate. In the real world, that is not easily done. See chapter 11 for the nuts and bolts of the horrible-schools debate, although it's not much of a debate. Too many children are stuck in hideous, awful places—not rave concerts or rap festivals or modern art museums—called schools.

A segment of the population will *never* see teachers in a positive light:

- Parents who believe teachers have failed their children
- Adults who believe the majority of their own teachers failed them when they were kids

- People who voted for Ted Cruz
- Men and women who have worked tremendously hard in private industry or corporate America and who have, over the years, developed a deep-seated envy for employees in the public sector: this would also include resentment of firefighters, cops, and even DMV workers (if you can believe it)!
- Semi-literate and otherwise uneducated people who view anybody associated with education (or being highly educated) as an elitist: "I love the poorly educated!"—Donald Trump
- Other teachers who view popular teachers as a threat or condemn mediocre teachers for falling below their own sets of standards
- Other teachers who don't handle things the way *they* would handle things with their own students: "I can't believe your teacher won't let you make up that test! I would. I always let my students make up tests after they have been absent!"
- People who believe most teachers are child-molesting, child-abusing, lecherous scumbags [13]

Not much is going to offset the way these people think. In all aspects of policy development, there is a degree of critical thinking that takes place. If people fall short on meeting basic critical-thinking skills, we know one of three things: (1) They are emotionally vested in the subject, and their critical thinking pales in comparison to their emotions. (2) They are not operating with a full deck of cards to begin with. (3) They have attended America's public schools.

It is inherently impossible to alter the thinking in certain segments of the population. Maybe a more emotional, visceral plea would help: focus on teacher *commitment*, that vast majority of teachers who come to their jobs every day, work hard, and love what they do.

It is particularly important not to confuse this focus with an obsession with movie teachers, or those rhapsodized in *Waiting for Superman*. The impracticality of actually waiting for Superman thwarts any hope we have of respecting our teachers for who they really are or for the marvelous things they are doing for our children.

NOTES

1. John Dean (Whittier College), *Teaching in the Secondary School,* Course Lecture #1, August, 1973.
2. Those three labels aren't so bad: rebellious, angry, insecure; in fact, that shows teachers have some fight in them. But the media, politicians, and public portray teachers as lazy, incompetent, and lecherous. Now, *that's* bad.
3. Health and Education Research and Operative Services, "Project Star: Tennessee's K–3 Class Size Study," 2009, www.heroes-inc.org/star.htm. This study approached determining the

effectiveness of smaller class sizes in grades K–3 on several different levels, using a number of methodologies. The results showed the overall benefits of smaller class sizes and the mental and emotional benefits to educators.

4. Michelle Manno, "The Highest and Lowest Teachers' Salaries in the U.S.," *Teach: Make a Difference*, October 20, 2014.

5. So-called progressive positions on issues have been a mainstay of teacher unions—but not of teachers. Most rank-and-file teachers probably would describe themselves as middle-of-the-road, with almost an equal number leaning to the left or the right, although more teachers would probably identify themselves as being on the left.

6. Richard Berman, "The Truth about Teachers Unions," *Orange County Register*," March 24, 2016, Local Section, 11.

7. Ibid.

8. Most people would probably agree that the original version of *West Side Story* was sanitized enough that the sex and violence were mere suggestions, rather than graphic depictions. However, by comparison, the characters in the original ABC television sitcom *Leave It to Beaver* were too antiseptic to be true; thus, the comparative reference here.

9. Bruce Gevirtzman, *Audacious Cures for America's Ailing Schools* (Lanham, MD: Rowman & Littlefield, 2011), chapter 2 (summary of).

10. What about Swiss cheese *on* sliced bread? Hmm . . . ?

11. Maureen Sullivan, "The Surprising Impact That Common Core Is Already Making on Schools," *Forbes*, February 29, 2016, Education Section, 1.

12. The World According to Opa, "Why I Am Against School Vouchers," October 7, 2007, https://kgarry.wordpress.com/2007/10/07/why-i-am-against-school-voucher-programs/.

13. The people who think this—and even voice it—are the people who motivated me to come to the defense of America's teachers. The number of teachers who carry on this kind of despicable activity is minuscule. But it only takes one. And if your kid is abused by that "one," the fact that the number is so tiny becomes irrelevant, even a potential source of anger. See chapter 12.

Chapter Eight

One Size Does Not Fit All

This is the sleeping giant.

People don't listen. No one seems to care. If they did, reforms would be made. Most teachers would be happier. Life would be easier. And our children would frolic to their futures, their enthusiasm unabated, their lives filled with success. In fact, our planet—nay!—our entire universe would be seated in the center of *perfect*.

Ready?

Here goes...

People are different.

Unfortunately, educators have not recognized this tidbit. Or maybe it is the political leadership of our nation that has been bemused by the differences in individuals, especially when it comes to how they learn. Parents have played that role, too. Often parents have embraced the mindset that their own children are, well, who *they* are, and everyone else's child must be exactly that way, too.

Or maybe it's the reverse: *My kid is who he is. There is none other like her. And my child is as close to perfect as anyone else is going to get*; hence, the belief that most *other* kids are the same. But the unique one is mine. (*That* "unique" often being better, because, as most people reluctantly admit, some unique kids wear horns or have nicknames like *Lucifer*.)

To un-jumble this mess, consider ways in which teachers—and by association, their students—have had to suffer the indignities of the cookie-cutter approach to education. It's baffling that adults, well educated, supposedly brilliant men and women, have come over so far to the other side of the moon.

Chapter 8

The Nature of the Cookie-Cutter

Had parents figured it out, they would have been steaming-hot mad about what's happening in education. They would have organized a march on Washington. Maybe they once considered organizing that march after they'd finally had it with Michelle Obama's ruining their kids' school lunches. But this is worse. Far worse.

All kids don't learn the same way. (We know this: certainly, teachers hear this so often that they want to stumble out the doors of their respective faculty meetings and throw up.) But all teachers don't teach the same way, either. And guess what? All teachers don't approach the same curriculum with the same amount of enthusiasm, teaching prowess, or basic knowledge.

Some American literature teachers loathe the early-American stuff. Until they get to Thomas Paine, whose writings teach kids how important it is to shoot someone trying to break into their house, they find the early-American curriculum utterly tedious.

Amazingly, when they sit down with other English teachers, these teachers defend teaching works containing Native American hand signs and William Chase.[1] One might think they are talking about Babe Ruth and Joe DiMaggio, there is so much fire and enthusiasm lighting their eyes.

But when the old defenders of traditional literature explain to other teachers how much they enjoy teaching their students about the poetry of William Carlos Williams, or the short stories of F. Scott Fitzgerald, they see looks of disappointment on their faces. Banal references to their "old man" ways grow larger. Old age, to these teachers, has nothing to do with wisdom and everything to do with clownishness.

There is a difference of opinion about the value of certain pieces of literature. What could be so bad about that? Easy to fix—no?

Actually . . . *no.*

The trend is to go in the other direction, away from norms established by local school districts, or by the states. Much of America—okay, maybe not *much* of America, but a large enough portion of America that it receives what seems like an inordinate amount of attention—decries local control of education; in fact, a sizable segment of the leadership of this country denounces local control of *anything.* It wishes for the federal government to be involved in *everything.* And worse.

With perennially popular movements like Common Core and the International Baccalaureate, there tends to be a desire for a *one-world view* of, well, the world. This means, what is good enough for the goose is good enough for the gander. And *this* means, what's good enough for the kids in Geneva is good enough for the kids in Saratoga.[2]

But when educators step back . . . is it really?

A hodgepodge of teaching philosophies and mixes 'n' matches in curriculum continues. Educators are set back on their heels. The right hand doesn't know what the left hand is doing. And neither does the right brain know anything about the left brain. It's hit or miss, a shot in the dark; it's throwing out a lot of honey and hoping enough of it will attract the flies.

Things happen in education, and nobody knows, or understands, how or why they happened. It's a very weird thing. One day you're teaching Carl Sandburg's *Chicago* from a foul-smelling textbook you've utilized in your classroom for the past hundred years, and the next thing you know, you get a mandate from your department chairperson that claims you may no longer teach that poem; the poem is—get this—no longer going to be available because the textbook you have been using has been designated as *obsolete*! You ask her why this fine textbook is now obsolete, and you get a shrug or a wave of the arms from the person *who is supposed to be in charge of the curriculum*!

So, you go to the principal. You ask him the same question you asked your department chairperson, but you ask it in a different way: "Why am I now going to have make a hundred *copies* of Carl Sandburg's poem? The textbook I have been using since I came over here on a covered wagon has been taken away from me. What gives?"

The principal shrugs, too. But at least he mutters something about textbook alignment in the district. He explains that the bosses downtown have decided that the textbooks used in the eleventh-grade English curriculum are culturally insensitive: there are too many old dead white guys in that book. The district has decided—after several parent complaints—the way to go is for more cultural sensitivity. Which, in a nutshell, means you must change from using books with works of old dead white guys to using books with other authors: hip, cool writers, who may also be dead because they were killed in gang fights—who are from countries the kids can't pronounce, and the teachers can't locate on a map.

No matter how awful, banal, boring, confusing, irrelevant, or unimportant these authors' works are, writers like Whitman and Cummings and Sandburg will take a backseat to them. These authors have rarely been published in Western culture, at least not in the schools, and the new trend is for our children to decode them.

And it's more depressing than even *that*.

The cookie-cutter approach to education mandates that educators be on the same wavelength. That sounds desirable, until you realize that all teachers must be doing the same things at about the same time. Which means, if Bill's classroom in Los Angeles is reading "Song of Myself," by Walt Whitman, on or around December 15, Sarah's classroom in Pittsburgh is reading "Song of Myself," by Walt Whitman on or around December 15.

What's more—and probably worse—is that Mrs. Lankenshteil's classes in Hamburg must be reading "Song of Myself," by Walt Whitman on or around December 15. There is, technically and *literally*, a world full of "Song of Myself," by Walt Whitman, on or around December 15. In fact, the guy sitting in Switzerland is turning different shades of purple every time another folder full of Whitman's essays and projects comes in over his computer, especially because he didn't want to deal with another old dead white guy in the first place.

If the teacher complains that her students are not ready for the Whitman essay because they are still learning the fundamentals of essay structure and the basics of critical advocacy, the teacher may set herself up for a response that sounds something like this: *tough.*

The National Council of Teachers recently made some interesting findings from a survey of nearly one thousand teachers in the United States. The survey had to do with a teacher's self-perception. To a teacher, self-perception means a lot. *Perception* often is *reality*. To that teacher, reality and perception are the same thing.

Most teachers define themselves by their work. They also critically assess themselves in terms of what makes them effective with their students, or what causes them to reek around their students. Much of society, in and out of the education system, calls this "teaching style."

Educators give "teaching style" academic, collegiate attributes of, for example *lecturer*, *directive teaching*, or *facilitator*; regular people mainly know "teaching style" as whether a teacher yells and screams and turns red in the face a lot. It may also have quite a bit to do with how much homework a teacher assigns, especially on the weekends.

Here are five style categories: (1) easygoing, (2) strict and demanding, (3) entertaining, (4) involved and passionate, and (5) facilitator.

As a teacher, which of these would you prefer to be labeled? If you already are a teacher, which of these would you use to describe yourself?

Easygoing: I don't let everything slide; I merely look the other way in order to make the students' lives more manageable. These kids have it tough. I can accommodate them more than other people, including other teachers, think I can. And they *still* learn.

Strict and demanding: I am one ornery son-of-a-bitch! I load up my students with homework, and demand their assignments are turned in on time. If they are late with their work, or in getting to class, they are punished. I require my students to receive at least a 70 percent on tests in order for them to receive a passing grade.

Entertaining: Coming to my class is not unlike going to an amusement park—or a comedy club. There is plenty of excitement and adventure. My students find my sense of humor highly enjoyable, and they laugh a lot during class. You rarely hear my students complain of a dull moment. I take even the most boring material and make it come alive. I hold contests, game shows, and other forms of competition. I rarely show my students movies or other recorded material because I am much more interesting than those could ever be. I know this because my students tell me this is so.

Involved and passionate: Regular school hours do not constrain me. I hardly ever hear the bells ring; even if I heard the bells, I would ignore them. I love being at school. Oddly, I enjoy the kids. I like teenagers—or whatever the ages of the students in my classes. I spend money on school supplies and awards for student achievement. Whatever I teach, I find fascinating. Just the activity of learning makes me happy. When my students' faces magically light up because I have taught them something new or opened them up to a new concept or idea, I know I made the right choice in what to do with my life.

Facilitator: My primary job is to *assist* students in their learning. I do not spoon-feed my students information; I guide them as to where they may find information. I lead them to new ideas that they develop and share. I monitor them as they go through their learning modalities, in lieu of their figuring it out for themselves. By the end of the process, my students thank me for helping them, but not for telling them what to do and how to do it. I come from a relatively new breed of educators who have concluded that students learn better when they discover things for themselves.

Teachers in the survey[3] described themselves as follows:

1. easygoing: 10 percent
2. strict and demanding: 19 percent
3. entertaining: 11 percent
4. involved and passionate: 40 percent
5. facilitator: 20 percent

Easygoing and *entertaining* hogged a combined 21 percent of the respondent teachers. A certain style of teacher hangs his hat on his ability to entertain his students in a myriad of ways, not the least of which is to make them laugh a lot.

It's not surprising that about a fifth of the teachers think of themselves as strict. But a fifth also look at themselves as a facilitator. Most teachers used to look at themselves as, well, *teachers* and not warm bodies that merely facilitated their students. The guys in the supermarket who help people with groceries are facilitators. You don't need a license to do that.

It is comforting that 40 percent of the surveyed teachers thought of themselves as passionate and involved with their work. These are the teachers who put in lots of extra time with students, care about them, and act as though their curriculum matters.

Passion, not fear, is a key to good teaching. Knowledge of the subject matter helps, but a teacher who convinces her students that the lesson has some sort of relevance to their lives is a teacher the kids remember, and parents adore, because having that kind of teacher makes it so much easier for children to get up in the morning and go to school.

Teachers have been saddled with a philosophy to which the majority of them do not subscribe. They have sunk into a system that has not only perpetuated that philosophy but has also defended it hook, line, and sinker—in front of lawmakers, parents, and educators.

It may be common sense, it may be a no-brainer: Not all teachers should be teaching the same thing, the same way, at the same time. Yet, in many subjects and at almost all grade levels in the public schools, this is what they do.

When this delightful mode of teaching doesn't work—and it eventually doesn't—teachers catch most of the blame. It isn't as though *educators* catch most of the blame for instituting ludicrous policies; *teachers* get a bum rap. They are the fall guys. They live by the sword and die by the sword. The only problem is that the sword is handed to them. The color, make, model, and size of the sword are dictated to them. They have no say, no control. They complain a lot. Those lunchrooms in every school in America are filled with lugubrious obscenities that would make any drunken sailor blush.

Teachers must straddle a system that doesn't have the remotest chance of succeeding. The cookie-cutter approach to teaching kids is egregiously stupid; honestly, it does not require the wisdom of Solomon to know that.

Teachers do not like this! It is killing them, too! As it is ruining children, it is tearing teachers apart. They have lives. They have kids, too. Infrequently, they make demands, but the system won't flicker a sign of approval when teachers make demands. They are hesitant, scared—and wisely so.

1. *Teachers do not teach alike.*

While they *can* teach alike, for reasons already discussed, teaching alike is often counterproductive. One teacher's lecturing is not necessarily better than another teacher's facilitating. But those two teachers may be about as different in personality and knowledge as two teachers can possibly get. Teachers do not teach alike.

2. *Students do not learn alike.*

Some students like to sit still, go on task, and finish their work; others like to mess around in class and are capable of finishing their assignments when they get home. Some students like to move around the classroom; others, if they were forced to stand up in the middle of a crowded classroom, would have a tantrum. Some students like pictures; others like words. Some students like to hear; others like to see. Many students feel adequate only if they are allowed to put their hands on something, such as a chunk of clay that has been turned into a beautiful pot—or a chunk of clay that was a beautiful pot until a kid decided to launch it as a hand grenade; others lack the energy to touch anything—don't even want to move their hands or arms. Some students are motivated by hard-nosed directive teachers; others self-motivate, are rarely off task, and find inspiration from within.

Some students like to work in class and make good use of the time they have available to them; others prefer to take their work home where they can align their studies with other tasks they may have to perform or with frequent trips to raid the refrigerator. Some students take copious notes; others never write down anything yet manage to retain the essence of what they need to know for the test. Some students adore giving speeches; others would prefer to have taken the beach at Normandy. Some students like to read; others not only hate to read—they don't know how. Some students memorize anything that comes their way; others forget even their names. Some students ace tests; others blow chunks on tests.

Given this relatively small sampling of the learning differences among students, anyone who still thinks a one-size-fits-all approach in education is the best way to go comes off looking whacked.

3. A universal curriculum undermines American specialness.

America's educators tried internationalizing education through the International Baccalaureate program. That brilliant idea came into full fruition around fifteen years ago. At first, everyone cooed and smiled and liked the idea of challenging students while bringing them up to par with kids from countries like Finland. Except for those who didn't relish this advanced-studies program competing with Advanced Placement classes, most educators seemed to be hunky-dory with IB. But then a strange thing happened: IB began a tediously slow descent.

What happened?

The one-world view of education didn't patter away because Americans suddenly woke up one morning and wanted to take their country back. (Many would like to think *that* is what happened.) IB didn't float away into the sunset because teachers from Helsinki and Chicago couldn't find a common ground—much less a common language—in which to communicate. Many did have that problem; however, they quit the program, quit their jobs, or quit their lives.[4]

The IB program is fraught with inconsistencies, contradictions, and irrelevancies. But none of those are the reason for its imminent demise. International Baccalaureate pooped out when it came into conflict with another program, one that was covertly designed to achieve all of the goals and complete the tasks of IB, but would do so by combining with philosophies and educational jargon most educators could abide, understand. That program would send a message of one-worldliness, rigid standards, and American competitiveness—all at once—in the name of adaptation and change. America would, through this program, shed its veneer of unwillingness to cooperate with the advanced academics in Belgium and the liberal intellectuals in France.

America could have its cheeseburger and fondue . . . and eat it, too.

Common Core: the be-all and end-all.

The quality of Common Core clobbers the other mediocre, flash-in-the-pan programs that preceded it. But the earlier programs relied on local jurisdiction to mess up the schools even further, instead of federal administration, which holds up scary-looking bureaucrats and dares educators to defy them.

Within the education community, there is divisiveness over Common Core. Some love it. Some hate it. Most are confused by it. And those who are confused do not admit to their confusion. The fragmentation of Common Core bewilders almost every educator in the United States, whether those educators—that certain percentage in denial—admit to their confusion or not.

Here are the primary drawbacks to Common Core.

1. Jeb Bush supported Common Core during the brief period of time he was running for president.

Although his praise for Common Core wasn't the major reason for Governor Bush's demise in the 2016 Republican primary season, Jeb Bush extolled the virtues of Common Core. Others, like Donald Trump and Marco Rubio, pounced on Jeb, and the ex-governor wound up getting several black eyes for backing an education program that he truly didn't give one pimp about. Donald Trump maligned Common Core but didn't know what Common Core was. This could be good *or* bad, but most people aren't sure. Suffice it to say that it depends on what you thought about Donald Trump.

2. A lack of understanding of Common Core persists.

Common Core is not this huge, monolithic program that consumes anyone or anything that comes near it. It is a federal-state program. Its purpose is to set standards, mostly uniform, for student achievement. Not all states comply. The federal government can punish financially, which it has not done and probably won't. Mostly educators are in control of Common Core standards. There are unusual—albeit, weird—twists and alterations of curriculum in English and mathematics, but supporters of Common Core swear until they go to their graves—some have already gone there—that Common Core's main goal is student achievement, but in a practical, applicable-to-the-real-world sensibility.

2. *Common Core's detractors are loud and proud in their criticisms.*

Marion Brady, a teacher, and Patrick Murray, an elected member of the school board in Bradford, Maine, wrote that Common Core drains initiative from teachers and enforces a "one-size-fits-all" curriculum that ignores cultural differences among classrooms and students.[5] (Hmm . . . that sound familiar?) Diane Ravitch, former U.S. assistant aecretary of education and education historian, wrote in her book *Reign of Error* that the Common Core standards were never field-tested and that no one knows whether they will improve education.[6]

Nicholas Tampio, assistant professor of political science at Fordham University, said that the standards emphasize rote learning and uniformity over creativity and fail to recognize differences in learning styles. Moreover, he points out that teachers' styles vary, and a good teacher must teach according to his own style. For example, if the teacher is an excellent lecturer, that teacher is hindered when told to allow students more time to self-actualize or discuss complex concepts among themselves.[7]

Teachers must have the flexibility to teach the way they do best. Students must be allowed to learn in ways that suit them individually. Common sense, no? One would think so. But there are a lot of things going on in American education that defy common sense. Many of them revolve around Common Core.

3. *The public hates Common Core.*

And this is a riot: they don't understand it! They hate it and they don't understand it! Some teachers hate Common Core, and they don't understand it, either. A fair guess is that the men and women who developed Common Core don't understand it; and they hate it by now, too. This is hysterical! Everybody hates Common Core—or they *say* they do because it is the correct thing to say—but they don't get it. Maybe they've read about it, heard about it, watched presidential debates in which the plaudits for or evils of Common Core were discussed, but they do not understand Common Core.

Which is all extremely weird, because Common Core isn't that tough to understand. Again: Common Core is a system, based on learning and assessment, in which federal standards are set for student learning in the public schools. That's pretty simple. Maybe too simple an explanation, but that is basically the idea: clear standards for student achievement, rigorous study, and common areas of assessment.

Oh, yeah, there are extenuating factors and possible quirks that may make Common Core unclear to some people, including teachers, but they aren't that big a deal; in some cases, they are actually good things. But what happens is that new misconceptions get circulated, people argue for and defend against it, political leanings get interjected into the conversation, and something like Common Core develops into the evil bully everyone is afraid of. And teachers catch the blame.

Teachers have been saddled with Common Core for the last seven years. They have defended it *and* hated it. But one thing is clear ... well, maybe there isn't one thing clear about this program. Here are the main topics concerning Common Core that get people riled up. See if things are so awful.

1. Universal application

This typically means *national* applications. But there are international standards and jargon here, as well, especially when it comes to math and science. More than just a few people have expressed their views on this subject. Sue, a teacher, said, "The standards are ridiculously developmentally inappropriate. It couches desired outcomes as abstract skills to be attained rather than in terms of world knowledge—knowledge of what—and specific procedural knowledge—knowledge of how. The focus on [international] informational text and close reading is ridiculous."[8]

Too much international is dismaying, as is none at all.

2. National standards

Common Core mandates national education standards—minimum standards—to which all states must aspire. Each state may reach for the stars, but must formulate minimum standards in math, science, and English. A *minimum*: every kid must be able to count to ten. *Reach for the stars*: every kid must be able to count to a hundred. Now, those are some distant stars!

3. Real-life applications

Common Core places an emphasis on the value of the learning: the importance for the child in her own life ... now. If she studies *Death of a Salesman*, she will discover more than the many motifs and symbolisms achieved by Arthur Miller; in fact, the reader might learn how to adjust her definition of the American Dream—and, therefore, the kind of man she eventually will seek to marry, or the type of career she will ultimately want for herself. An honest teacher using the Common Core might carry on a conversation with a student that goes something like this:

>STUDENT: So, why do we gotta learn this play?
>TEACHER: You don't like it?
>STUDENT: It sucks.
>TEACHER: And why does it suck?

STUDENT: 'Cuz it's hard to read and seems pointless.
TEACHER: What if I helped you with the play and explained the point of it?
STUDENT: That's boring then!
TEACHER: We don't read this, or any other literature, in my class because it's thrilling. We read it for what it can do for our lives . . . and for our world. If I show you how what we read can make your own life better and maybe improve the world around you a little bit, would it be worth it to you to suffer through a little boredom?[9]

The student doesn't respond. He sits with his mouth agape.

Now, that is a component of Common Core: making the literature or the math have relevance.

4. An emphasis on technique

Proponents of Common Core claim that it isn't merely arriving at the correct answer that demonstrates competency in a subject area; it is the *process* by which someone arrives at that correct—or incorrect—answer that makes a difference.

The emphasis on technique and process is especially important in math. If two and two are four, how did we get to the *four*? Logically, if you can get to the *four* through a process you have mastered, you can get to *any* answer for any problem once you have mastered that process or, at least, demonstrated the ability to venture through that process with some confidence and fluency. It's sort of like asking the *why* for any answer to a question. People should not be satisfied with only the answer; the method of arriving at that answer winds up as more crucial than the answer itself.

Some Common Core math teachers are unhappy about supplying answer sheets to homework problems, thinking a student will copy answers and then play video games or watch *Sponge Bob*. But a good Common Core math teacher evaluates her students through how they handle the process. *Show your work. Show your work. Show your work.* Just how many times have schoolchildren heard this mantra?

Betty went to visit her daughter's sixth-grade math teacher. Betty's daughter, Elsa, struggled in math. Betty couldn't handle the math, either. She understood most of the math while she was in school, but when she got to high school, her math skills were clearly waning. Betty is a smart woman, but some of the complex equations and graphs became too much for her.

Elsa's teacher said calmly, "Your daughter understands the concepts. She usually gets the right answers. That's not the problem. The right answers are not the problem."

"Then what's the problem?" Elsa's mother asked, a little confused.

"The problem," the math teacher explained, "is that Elsa doesn't show her work. I don't know if she understands how she got to the place she went to."

"But she got to that place?" Betty asked.

"Yes," the teacher nodded, "she got to the right place. But in order to assure me that she knows how to get to the right place in the future, she must show her work. What I ask the students to do is use a single side of a whole sheet of paper to show how they calculated the problem. So, if they do ten problems, they are required to show their work on five sheets of paper."

Betty didn't understand the math that the teacher used to explain his requirements for helping Elsa do better in his class. But she got the main point: Elsa had to show her calculations to the teacher. Those calculations had to be neat and clear, and using a spacious area on the paper would guarantee this.

The computation was more important than getting the correct answers; it was more important than being perfect on the upcoming exams that would cover each unit. And it was more important than the workers at McDonald's getting Betty's order right when she used the drive-through window.

Despite the fact that Betty was aware of the teacher's professional commitment to the new Common Core math implementation, the teacher's impatience with her daughter generated feelings of resentment in Betty. Shaking her head, she crossed her arms and said to Elsa, "Your teacher is an idiot."

Your teacher doesn't know what he's talking about.
You teacher is lousy.
Your teacher doesn't know how to teach.
Your teacher is a jerk.
Your teacher needs to go back to school.
Your teacher is behind the times.
Your teacher is too strict.
Your teacher is too easy.

The criticisms abound. Teachers can't win from losing. Politicians pass legislation that directly affects their performance in the classroom—and to a large extent, the entirety of their lives—and teachers are expected to adapt and perform. The legislation brings programs and fads and philosophies that may not be worthy of their endeavors, but that doesn't matter. Common Core, No Child Left Behind, Second to None, programs through which educators, and noneducators, believe they have found the panacea, a perfect way of solving our nation's ills, eventually wind up in the scrap heap of worthless education jargon.

It is as though the so-called experts—the researchers—are claiming that they have found the cure for cancer; yet the doctors who actually see and treat patients know these experts are wrong. The doctors still want to use traditional forms of treatment. Yes, these treatments have not solved the problem; and, yes, these treatments still leave a lot to be desired. But there are variations of these treatments that should not be discarded in favor of that which is unproven and, perhaps, counterproductive.

The doctors believe they can be successful because (1) much of what they have utilized to fight cancer is tried and proven and (2) they are still passionate and enthusiastic in their daily routines and frequent contacts with their patients.

Many will say this is a variation on the, "You can't teach an old dog new tricks" philosophy: wickedly bad for medicine, similarly awful for education. *Hey, man, everything you have been doing so far is wrong! Try something new already!*

Educators *have* tried new. Common Core is new. In the last twenty years, there has been a minimum of (depending upon how one defines this) eight well-publicized movements in education, with previous programs thoroughly gutted and redefined. The most recent, No Child Left Behind, has been, thankfully, left behind. Education reforms are necessary. On an ongoing basis, changes should be made. But requisites of flexibility, accountability, and satiability have to be incorporated in any reform that encompasses the entire education community and all of its students.

When these reforms fall short, and to date, they always have fallen short, the general trend is to single out America's teachers as the main cause of the programs' demise. Admittedly, some teachers chomp it; they stink. But as a whole, when reforms and ideas are thrown out there, and force all teachers to comply with a rigidity they have never before experienced, teachers are often thrown off their game. Like doctors required to apply medical treatments they are not comfortable using, teachers who must teach with styles that are not flattering to them, or curricula that do not suit them, have been set up to fail.

Even after all this, the majority of teachers have risen from the ashes—victorious. They have done their jobs. They have discovered tools of disengagement, a separation from gloom and doom, and found a way to mold the lives of kids by advancing information and values necessary for them to flourish.

What happens? *Other* factors, circumstances and conditions out of the teacher's control, rear their ugly heads. Drugs and alcohol and gangs violate the community. Broken homes and dysfunctional families replace the normalcy of years gone by. Advancing technologies that *detract* from the educational process, such as smartphones and video games, occupy extraordinary numbers of hours in a child's day. Religion and other positive social outlets for young people have disappeared.

But the teacher continues to work under those conditions, somehow adapting to one-size-fits-all, international mandates of London, and an onslaught of bureaucracy from Washington, DC.

Those teachers! Don't they know that all kids aren't alike! You'd think by now . . .

Teachers want out of this. They do. If you've read the story "The Emperor's New Clothes,"[10] you may understand what it's like to be in education. You nod and smile and acquiesce to each new mandate. But you know. You know the truth. If you're a teacher, you know the truth—and that truth may bury you.

NOTES

1. William Merritt Chase was an American painter, known as an exponent of Impressionism and as a teacher. Studying him must be a thrilling ride for any modern teenager.

2. IB Foundation Office, Geneva Switzerland, http://www.ibo.org/en/contact-the-ib/office-locations/ib-foundation-office-geneva/: founded in 1968, and mushrooming around the turn of the millennium.

3. Standards Council Conference, Glenbrook, IL, 1997. Not to be confused with a teachers union doodad. This group was one of the first to adapt curriculum to methods, while looking at various national standards for secondary education in the United States. Eventually, the states, which finally *showed* some balls, took their balls home and tried setting standards for themselves, resulting in an uneven and somewhat tedious system.

4. The program is still popular in the midwestern states. Some state universities, however, have stopped giving IB equal weight with AP classes.

5. "Common Core Corruption," *Red Nation Rising*, January 23, 2015, https://rednationrising.wordpress.com/2015/01/23/common-core-corruption/.

6. Ibid.

7. Ibid.

8. "Common Core: Five Teachers Open Up, and They Don't Hold Back," *Yahoo News*, January 23, 2016, par. 15, https://www.yahoo.com/news/common-core-5-teachers-open-up-1348959887343670.html.

9. This is where it can get tenuous. The teacher may start taking about poets like William Carlos Williams or novelists like Stephen Crane. One has to be suspicious when this occurs.

10. "The Emperor's New Clothes," by Hans Christian Andersen, could be a classic metaphor for what's happening in education. In the story, of course, the emperor did not have new clothes. He was naked.

Chapter Nine

Making the Grade

Dumb people dominate the earth.

Okay, maybe not. But how about this: dumb people exist everywhere on the planet.

That's better: it's more accurate. Dumb people may not *dominate* the earth, but they do exist everywhere. They inhabit all professions. Jerry used to think that his neighbor Jackson was the smartest guy in the world. Jackson managed a computerized chemical plant. His job was to make things right in rubber and fiber technology, *as it applied to the manufacture of spacecraft*!

How about them apples!

More to the point: How about that guy and the rubber plant! If he can mix a bunch of chemicals together and come up with fiber capable of being used in spacecraft (What does that even *mean*?), he must be one smart cookie, right?

Wrong.

Jackson did stupid things all the time; in fact, he entangled himself in so many messes that he repeatedly referred to *himself* as *stupid*! Jackson bought a sailboat at what he thought was a pretty good price; unfortunately, when he discovered how much money it would take to dock the boat, he wound up selling it at a loss. He could have paid three months mortgage with that loss!

Jackson also gave an old girlfriend a brand-new car for her birthday. He figured, with some luck, her ecstasy over the car would throw her right back into his arms. Nope. She became angry with him over his lack of punctuality when delivering the car and tried to run him over with it in the driveway of her home. He never saw her again after that.

Not too swift upstairs, huh?

Oh, by the way: in addition to Jackson's rubber/fiber thing, he boasted of graduating from Cal Poly University in Pomona, with a degree in the computer sciences. No doubt, at least on paper, Jackson wielded some pretty impressive credentials when it came to appearing smart. So, how could someone seemingly brilliant turn out to be such a dunce?

How? It happens all the time. Smarts appearances do not necessarily equate to logical behavior or practical aptitude. Most teachers look smart . . . on paper. And some look pretty dumb on paper. Before delving into an analysis of how smart or learned a teacher should be, consider ten of the most important characteristics of a good—or even great—teacher. In fact, leave it at *great*. Don't fiddle with mediocrity here. Revolving a defense of America's teachers by proving they are, at the very least, mediocre does not exactly jolt the American people into a wild-eyed respect for America's educators.

Great teachers:

- Love their jobs
- Like to be around kids
- Know how to teach
- Lead balanced lives
- Fake it when they have to
- Embrace the new technology
- Understand what is truly important in life
- Make their subjects come alive
- Go above and beyond the call of duty
- Control their impulses
- Prefer cats to dogs

Oh, gosh darn! What about . . . *experts in their subject matter*? Is it not simply a given that great teachers would be true experts in the subjects they are teaching America's kids?

Teachers can't be dummies in their subject areas. How would it look, a middle school math teacher who can't add fractions when the denominators are of different numbers?

But teachers don't have to possess doctorates in their subjects in order for them to teach their subjects.

The higher on the education pyramid in the public schools a teacher climbs, the deeper he should submerge himself in the subjects he teaches. A history teacher, for example, who is instructing high school juniors in the details of Advanced Placement U.S. History had better be knowledgeable about the Civil War; his proficiency in the content material should speak for itself as soon as he moves to prepare complex lessons and in-depth analysis for his students; when he moves to the lectern to present material, no one entertains the slightest doubt he stands on top of his game.

The presentation of Native American customs to fifth graders requires only a rudimentary level of course content proficiency on the part of the elementary school teacher. But a fourth-grade teacher better know how to present the material in ways that will both inform and entertain the little tykes who sit before her, their paws endlessly slipping into their backpacks in order to search for the cell phones that have been forbidden by their teachers and school administrators.

Clearly, the criteria for being labeled a great teacher change with the setting and situation. In general, the higher the grade level, the less emphasis is placed on teaching skills and strategies of presentations to students, and more importance is relegated to the teacher's knowledge in the subject area. College requires a little less teaching strategy and more content mastery. The lower the grade level, the fewer content details and information required of the teacher, but more in the way of presentation and teaching strategies come into play.

That said, teacher intelligence and competency are denigrated every once in a while—maybe too often. It is intriguing that hardly anyone questions a teacher's ability to teach, but criticism is often leveled at a teacher's comprehension and knowledge of what he is teaching. More often than not, teachers are incompetent because they don't know how to properly relate and disperse the subject to their students, not because they don't have a clue what they are talking about.

A few comments about these matters are echoed often; they need to be handled: *Dumb teacher! Billy's teacher is stupid; stupid people should not be teaching!*

Stupid people *don't* teach. Oh, sure, every once in a while, a simpleton sneaks into the teaching ranks, but consider the subjective nature of labeling someone else, especially a professional, as "stupid."

People often use the word *stupid* to mean qualities other than *stupid*: mean, ill advised, cruel, misinformed, or reprehensible. *Stupid*, in its purest form, means a lack of intelligence. Intelligence is measured—at least typically—by IQ level. Teachers' IQs are rarely, if ever, taken. Therefore, there has to be another objective means of determining someone else's intelligence level, right?

Anecdotal examples exist; however, if most people had their intelligence levels measured by isolated examples of the dumb things they have done, almost everyone—probably *everyone*—would be considered stupid.

Other factors provide evidence for determining if America's teachers are stupid.

1. Teachers have completed significantly high levels of education.

The overall education statistics for teachers who have been placed in America's classrooms are quite impressive. A whopping 1.8 million public school teachers have a master's degree or better, which is roughly 54 percent of the total number of teachers.[1]

2. Teachers, generally, have exercised sound judgment.

Much of this book has been dedicated to discussing areas in which teachers have *not* exercised solid judgment. But considering just how *many* decisions teachers must make, day in and day out, it is astounding that human beings are capable of holding down the education fortress that protects America's kids from the possible follies that would ensue without those protections.

Teachers make decisions all day in areas that most people would find massively intimidating: grading, program expansion, counseling children, dealing with parents, curriculum, instructional standards, special committees, training, lesson plans, whom to blame for their own lack of success (a little joke there), and so on. It's not easy. Most teachers must simultaneously take on the roles of cop, parent, and, well, teacher. Sometimes it's tough knowing which of these come into play in a given situation.

Teachers are hardly ever complimented for playing these multifaceted roles, but they are readily indicted for blowing any one of them when they make a mistake.

Mr. Barber: the most popular social studies teacher at a high school where he taught for over twenty-five years. Mr. Barber knew his stuff. He was always highest on the lists of his students' favorite teachers. He won several teaching commendations, including "Teacher of the Year" for his entire school district in 2012. He chaperoned dances, volunteered to be a ticket taker at Friday night football games, and acted as advisor for several clubs on campus, including a nationally ranked Academic Decathlon team.

But Mr. Barber made a mistake—a big one. It was not an ill-motivated error; he had a lapse in judgment. Some referred to Mr. Barber's decision as a "brain fart." And if that were truly the case, it was the fart heard "round the world"—or, at least, heard "round the town."

Mr. Barber gave one of his female students a ride home from school. He saw her dragging her backpack along the street; he stopped and asked her if she wanted some help, and the girl gratefully accepted. They went right to her home. He pulled to the curb; they said their farewells, and Mr. Barber drove away.

The next morning, about an hour after the first school bell had rung, the city police interrupted Mr. Barber's class lecture. The cops, many of whom knew Mr. Barber personally, barged into his classroom, grabbed the history teacher, and handcuffed him in front of his students, those he had been teaching for almost a full school year. Mr. Barber, completely bewildered, fell to the floor, as two policeman pounced upon him and violently dragged him to his feet. His students, mystified, were also frightened—shocked—by what they witnessed. The scene had become surreal.

Unbeknownst to Mr. Barber—you can guess the story here, what transpired—the female student whom he had given a brief ride to ruined Mr. Barber's life that afternoon. Evidently, she had gotten some poor academic news from one of her teachers earlier in the day. Coincidently, she had witnessed her boyfriend holding hands with another girl during lunch. To say the least, the girl's mood soured. Dropping her backpack to the ground, she walked by herself along the street.

Angry and depressed, resigned to her miserable personal and academic fates, she gathered together some sort of personal redemption when Mr. Barber, one of her favorite teachers, kindly gave her a ride home, a respite from her own thoughts and personal misery.

But when she walked into the house, glum and disheveled by the tormenting events of the day, her angry parents pounced upon her. The math teacher had called her parents and told them of their daughter's failing grade. Upon trying to absorb her parents' wrath, she withdrew to her bedroom and cried.

That was the moment she impulsively decided the only way she could bear the anguish of her day was to accuse her history teacher of a vile act—and, oh, she thought, not too vile, not really—that could reasonably explain her pained emotional outbursts.

She claimed Mr. Barber had been flirting with her for several days. He leaned over to give her a kiss on the mouth. Of course, she said, she had resisted his advance. But it was enough to rattle her, to upset her, to put her in an awful blood-sucking mood. Up until that point, his flirting had grossed her out, caused her to lose concentration in her classes, and cost her a boyfriend; she had taken her nervousness out on him, not on Mr. Barber.

The girl was convincing when the police questioned her; the cops decided to arrest Mr. Barber. It was a tough call; after all, Mr. Barber had been a good egg for so long, forever really, and had built up a moral bank account. But even a moral bank account as huge as the one accumulated by Mr. Barber could not survive an accusation of molestation by a teacher, however spontaneous and unsubstantiated and circumstantial.

Immediately after, and in subsequent days, the following rumors and comments were floated about—around the community, in the newspapers, and on the high school campus where Mr. Barber had taught:[2]

- *I always had my suspicions about Mr. Barber. He just seemed too nice. Maybe he was a little naïve.*
- *Dumb ass. It was probably not the way she said, but he's a dumb ass for letting her get into his car.*
- *Mr. Barber is a lot more stupid than I thought.*

- *Whether the girl's allegations are true or not, the veteran teacher did not exercise sound judgment.*
- *For a talented teacher so seemingly brilliant, Mr. Barber chose a path of self-destruction* (even if the girl had lied about his aggressive advances).
- *What a dick!* (Not sure what that means, but it's probably not good. At best, that word wrongfully replaces the word *stupid*; they do not mean the same thing.)
- *Stupid! I've met a lot of stupid teachers in my day, and this guy is also a dick!*[3]

Admittedly, some of these people don't come off as the brightest bulbs on the Christmas tree. But Mr. Barber doesn't appear to be all that sharp, either. When it comes to names and dates and places that had impact on the founding of the United States of America, Mr. Barber is probably the smartest guy in the room. When teachers are gauged by their talent to disperse these names and dates and places, and make them important in the hearts and minds of the nation's youth, Mr. Barber wins that contest hands down.

But Mr. Barber loses big-time in the common sense department. One lapse in judgment, whether intentional or not, whether the consequences of the act had serious detrimental effect on the girl or not, portrays him as a guy you can't trust to be a teacher, not because he really made advances toward the girl, but because he willfully put himself into a position to be accused of such a dastardly deed.

By the way: less than three weeks later, the girl in question broke into a tearful confession that she had made the whole story up; after all, too many bad things had happened to her that day, and her parents' attitude was the last straw! She apologized to Mr. Barber. But the teacher's career had already received a punishing blow.

Remember, this is an isolated example of bad judgment by a teacher. By and large, maybe 99 percent of the time, America's teachers say, and do, the right thing.[4]

3. Teacher training works.

America's schoolteachers receive education and training on several different levels and during various times in their career:

Teachers go to school in order to become teachers.

And the road is rigorous. America's education colleges and undergraduate programs in education vary state by state, but no states give prospective teachers a free pass. It would be political suicide to do so.

Some states—and colleges—test teacher competency even before they receive a BA degree!

Teachers must take at least one year (usually more) of undergraduate courses.

These courses normally have to do with advanced classes in the student's major area of study, the one in which she will eventually become credentialed to teach. But they also connect future teachers to studies in teaching methods, curriculum, and education philosophy. It is no secret that budding young teachers despise most of these courses; they are often difficult and present obstacles to becoming a certified teacher. Teaching is an art. It is at the graduate level where young people begin painting their own canvas.

Teachers must do at least a semester of student teaching.

This means under the direction, and control, of a qualified master teacher, who is paid for his supervision by either the school district or by the college from which the student teacher came. Sometimes a master teacher is paid to supervise student teachers by both sources.

Most student-teaching assignments are from five to ten months long. Students are not paid for their work; in fact, in most instances, *they* must pay the college, because student teaching is another three-credit or six-credit course they are compelled to take. Master teachers observe their students while they teach classes.

Eventually, the master teacher has to feel comfortable enough to leave the classroom under the student teacher's control. This is why many veteran teachers enjoy having student teachers. It can be a pretty good gig. Besides getting paid to supervise, master teachers can go to the bathroom for a change, or have a Coke in the faculty lounge.

Supervising teachers submit detailed written evaluations of their student teachers. Less often, master teachers are required to do a verbal evaluation in front of a college committee. Sometimes the master teacher is responsible for assigning the actual grade the student will receive in the course.

Down the road, it is the master teacher who is asked to submit letters of recommendation for possible teaching positions for which their students have applied. Writing this letter is an enormous responsibility. Master teachers may simply opt out of the evaluation process for a number of reasons, not the least of which is that their consciences won't allow them to recommend the Bozo they just worked with to teach kids.

Sometimes master teachers *do* write negative recommendation letters. A negative letter could kill a prospective teacher's chances of entering the job force before she enters it. She may resort to looking for work as the custodian who cleans up the messes at places like the Republican National Convention.

4. Teachers are irreplaceable.

People who don't know any better often ask a question like this: *Why can't smart, college educated people who work in business go into the public schools and teach? They can teach higher level math, science, and computer technology. They would certainly be qualified to offer their experience and wisdom to business students. What would be better than that?*

Truthfully, a lot of things would be better than that.

Professionals already work hard.

What would they have left to give schoolchildren? The retired ones: Just how old would they be when they started a teaching career? It's almost as though our kids would get the leftovers from a long and delicious meal.

Many professionals hold biases against kids.

If a professional software programmer itched with an intense desire to be around smiley, happy school children, she might have chosen a different profession when she actually had the chance to do so . . . like schoolteacher, for example. A large number of adults can't stand kids: many don't know how to treat them or act around them; others would rather have been in New Orleans during Katrina than work with a bunch of teenagers.

Teacher colleges breed special people: *teachers*. Not everyone is cut out to be one because those who are not teachers are probably not teachers for a myriad of reasons: hating kids may be one of those reasons. Some people grow up and get married, and they never have children. They don't *want* them. In the old days, landlords who owned apartment buildings and houses refused to rent to people who had children of any age. This is illegal now. But society once reckoned with the notion that some people are better off nowhere in the vicinity of creepy, crawly small ones. They drool. They pass gas. And those are the parents. The young ones are almost as bad.

Actually, that's wrong. The older kids are worse. They also can be dangerous. Have you ever been in a Burger King at night when three or four teenagers walked in the door? Want to call the National Guard, don't you?[5]

For a variety of reasons, albeit one or two of them completely unfounded, a certain number of Americans have chosen to stay away from the teaching profession because it involves spending the majority of their waking day around young people. These individuals have smartly sought employment in specializations—or just plain old jobs—in which there are few, or no, children present. Now there are those who advocate calling them outside their comfort zones and asking them to walk naked into our nation's classrooms.

Professionals don't know how to teach.

Of course, cynics contend that teachers don't know how to teach, either.

On the surface—the very *top* of that surface—the idea of smart adults who are experts in their fields teaching children what they know sounds reasonable. But here's the rub: the key word is *teaching*. It is one thing to *know* and quite another thing to *teach* what you know. Grant Baker said, "I find it utterly insulting that millions of teachers have passed through billions of hours of education, to the tune of hundreds of billions of dollars, and there are those who would wave it off with a flick of the wrist and say, 'That's okay, you can teach without all that. Just walk right in!'"[6]

Just walk right in: with no tools for how to do it. It would be like a really smart and learned man walking into the bathroom with the intent of repairing the pipes leading to the city's sewers. One would think this guy would need a wrench or something, but he doesn't have one. Still, he expects to get the job done. Why? Because others have reassured him that he is smart enough and knows about the community's plumbing system.

Professional teachers have taken years and years to learn their craft from others who have done it before them. They have practiced under expert guidance. They have been observed, evaluated, and retooled for their assignments. Some wind up doing it better than others. Some wind up not doing it well at all. But it is a process.

John Dewey, teacher educator, wrote, "Even though I taught middle and high school science, and had graduated with a Ph.D. in science education and geology, many . . . would agree that I couldn't possibly be prepared for all the challenges I would face in my new position. There is no question in my mind that the collaboration with colleagues over the years helped cultivate my identity and self-confidence in being and thinking like a teacher educator."[7]

To expect people who are not tooled to teach is insulting. But it's worse than insulting: it is stupid. It's worse than stupid. It's dangerous. This nation's future, perhaps its very existence, depends on our ability, and willingness, to teach our children. In the name of expediency or thrift, we should not skimp on our responsibilities in this important aspect of America's defense.

The following analogy evades the importance of having a well-educated and highly skilled citizenry, but it clarifies the point: If a Major League Baseball team were training to win the World Series, the club's owner would not hire a slew of elderly men to work with them in every aspect of the game, simply because those old men had once studied baseball and compiled offensive statistics for the Cleveland Indians. The people in charge of the Indians would hire men who had the experiences necessary to communicate effectively with the players.

Wouldn't they?

If not, they would be eliminated from the pennant race before the Fourth of July.

Just because the nerdy-looking guy with a bowtie who looks like the picture on the book covers of the *Dummies* series walks into a computer science room on a high school campus, it doesn't mean he is going to be able to impart much of anything to a bunch of squirmy, hormone-driven teenagers. We provide those skills for real teachers through:

1. Student teaching
2. Remedial training
3. Workshops
4. In-services
5. Administrator evaluations/observations
6. Conferences
7. Continuing higher-level education courses

That pontificating man in the dark suit who comes to us from the offices at IBM gets the benefit of none of those places. That's why he may know his subject matter but has no talent for teaching it to children.

5. Teachers are competent in their subject matters

The credentialing process makes it impossible for a teacher to be a dolt in his subject area. In some states, that process is blatantly grueling. Many states require minimum course requirements in graduate education. Some of those courses may be in the student's major, but others have nothing to do with his major: they are basics, in the foundations and the philosophies of education, as well as instruction in curriculum building, lesson planning, communicating with parents, and teaching methodologies.

Today's teachers are required to keep up with technological developments in education and are expected to demonstrate professional competency in computer technology. Teachers do not have to be software developers, but they must show they can use the software, especially if their districts have purchased a few trillion dollars–worth of various software products.

Some teachers say they feel pressure to use what they have learned about new technologies. And that may be true. But why would this be a bad thing? Carla, who retired in 2010, sighed and said, "I left teaching just in time. The year after I retired, teachers at my school were being required to enter their grades and assignment records *online!* They wanted teachers to have their own websites!"[8]

Oh, the humanity!

Teachers today constantly work extra hard just to keep up with the ever-growing changes in education. It is as though the teacher were being pushed rapidly through a revolving door. If she doesn't get out in time, the door will keep revolving. And she will get nowhere, for the moving door always comes back to its starting point.

Overall, teachers are one educated group of goofballs! Take *this*, you naysayers, you schools rippers! Bob Chase and Martin Gross reported *this:* "Let's look at the facts. Better than 99 percent of public-school teachers have at least a bachelor's degree. Beyond that, almost half of these teachers also have an advanced degree: 42 percent have a master's degree, 5 percent have specialized diplomas requiring at least one year of coursework beyond the master's level and about 1 percent have a doctorate. A recently released study by the Educational Testing Service, or ETS, concluded that 'teachers in academic subject areas have academic skills that are equal to or higher than those of the larger college-graduate population.'"[9]

These data shouldn't thwart the question: *Aren't there* any *unqualified teachers who are holding positions and teaching our children in the public schools*?

Just as there are unqualified police officers and doctors and car mechanics and massage therapists, there are unqualified teachers. *Overall*, the teaching profession brims with competency and talent.[10] Maligning teachers for that which they should be criticized is welcome. However, the constant battering of America's teachers for shortcomings only found in a very small number is not only counterproductive; it is immoral.

The berating of teachers by the general public and the media for that over which teachers have absolutely no control is a recipe for disaster: diversion to unsubstantiated and inaccurate accusations of incompetency and inadequacy leads to a failure to solve the real problems in education.[11]

In the O. J. Simpson murder case, the defense claimed O. J. Simpson is going to go out there and find the *real* killer! Unfortunately, that never happened. He didn't try. And there was no other "real" killer. In the case of our education establishment, however, there *are* real killers. If they are not found, tackled, and brought to remediation, they will kill again.

NOTES

1. "Private or Public Schools: Who's Ahead in Degrees?" *Face the Facts USA*, October 6, 2012, http://www.facethefactsusa.org/facts/private-or-public-schools-whos-ahead-by-degrees.

2. These are fictionalized accounts. Similar accusations, many of them unfounded, appear in newspapers every day. Naturally, students' names may not be used in media reporting, but the *teachers*' names can. Even if the teacher is cleared of all charges and goes free, as in the case of Mr. Barber, his life, for all intents and purposes, is over.

3. Maybe they do mean the same thing; at least, when they describe a teacher. Both terms are certainly pejorative.

4. Yeah, "maybe."

5. "Two Teens Arrested after Armed Robbery at Burger King with Airsoft Gun," WishTV.com, March 16, 2016, http://wishtv.com/2016/03/16/two-teens-arrested-after-armed-

robbery-at-burger-king-with-airsoft-gun/. Just to give some clarity to which most laypeople can't relate.

6. A national organization (with local affiliates) composed of retired teachers whose main lot in life, after several decades of teaching, is to sit around and bitch about things over which they no longer have any control.

7. S. M. Fishman and L. McCarthy, *John Dewey and the Challenge of Classroom Practice* (New York: Teachers College Press, 1998).

8. What Carla forgets to tell you is that websites had been required for teachers at her school for a couple of years before she retired. Time passed Carla by: badly.

9. Bob Chase and Martin L. Gross, "Insight on the News: Are America's Teachers Well-Qualified to Teach Our Children?" May 23, 2016, https://www.questia.com/magazine/1G1-57770446/q-are-america-s-teachers-well-qualified-to-teach.

10. Even with all the competency and the vast amount of talent in the teaching profession, the public and politicians are all too eager to dwell on the negative, just as they are with the police and doctors and, yes, lawyers. Very depressing.

11. Steven C. Ward, "Why Has Teacher Morale Plummeted?" *Newsweek*, April 10, 2015, Opinion Section. When these programs do not work, and they inevitably do not, teachers get blamed for it. The presumption being, *if you just knew how to teach, these programs, which we keep changing, would work! You dummies!*

Chapter Ten

Teachers Are People, Too

Mrs. Medina

In order for Mrs. Medina to walk to the back of her classroom, she had to slide through a maze of desks, backpacks, and feet. Her students, normally loud and springy, were preoccupied today.

In Mrs. Medina's senior English classes, composed of twelfth graders not bound for four-year colleges, this teacher is not a particularly dominant figure. Teachers normally control the focus in their classrooms. Mrs. Medina has a low profile. Normally, she does her job without much fanfare; her students are not particularly motivated to learn grammar, punctuation, and spelling, and Mrs. Medina is not altogether motivated to teach them—certainly nothing above and beyond the call of duty.

This morning feels slightly different. The atmosphere among the teenagers is filtered with apathy. The grind in a four-year comprehensive high school can take its toll. It has taken its toll on this class at Carver High School.

Many of the students have detached themselves from the importance of what lies ahead in the form of final exams. Mrs. Medina, well meaning and caring, has worn herself down trying to motivate her students to see the light at the end of the tunnel and to focus on the tasks at hand.

A couple of days ago, her doctor shocked Mrs. Medina with the news that she has advanced breast cancer.

Tomorrow she is scheduled to find out her own test results, those from her doctor. Based on a series of biopsies and tests checking for metastasis of the cancer, Mrs. Medina's doctor will let her know the severity of her disease, her overall prognosis. She will learn if the doctor thinks surgeons should remove her breast; she will hear news that could determine whether she could be expected to live for at least another five years or die within the year.

The preposterousness of this scene is only too clear after a student asks Mrs. Medina, "Does our final have a big effect on our grade?" Which, under normal circumstances, Mrs. Medina would shrug off and smile, while sarcastically quipping, "Not really. Your final test only tells me how much you have learned all semester. Why would that mean anything?"

But today Mrs. Medina nods and forces a smile. She wants her students to do well in life. But the omnipresent ennui in her classroom dooms the present gathering to mediocrity. Mrs. Medina cannot muster the courage to rise above her plight; her students could not initiate the enthusiasm to compensate for the teacher's sudden uselessness. These children are not self-motivated. What they have to accomplish would have been orchestrated by their English teacher; now, however, that end is impossible.

Flash! Bulletin!

Teachers are people, too.[1]

Teachers are born into this world as human beings first; then they turn into teachers. How that actually happens is not a mystery, though the process is not what matters most. Their ability to unite the two entities—human being and teacher—matters most. When teachers accomplish this feat, they have gathered for their identities the best of two worlds.

When teachers make mistakes, they should apologize. And most of them do. They apologize to their students; they apologize to their students' parents. They apologize to the site administrators, to the district's administrators, and sometimes they apologize to the entire community they serve. But that is rare. Teachers do not need to say, "I'm sorry" on a regular basis.

Mr. Jones

Randy Jones, a young and up-and-coming mathematics teacher, found his way to Garza Junior High School while working as an accounts manager at Bank of America. Initially, Randy earned his teaching credentials in mathematics because it was the best way to do what he was good at (working with numbers), with what he really *liked* to do (teach others about numbers). He liked the challenge of his position at the bank, and his salary was nothing to sneeze at, but Randy is a man who wants intimate interactions with people more than frigid interludes with graphics and charts.

"I like graphics and charts," Randy said.

But Randy liked people even more.

Did this liking for human beings extend to liking children, too? After all, some adults do not classify children as human beings.

Randy definitely was not one of those. When a boyhood friend of his, who just happened to be the principal at Garza Junior High School, mentioned to Randy at a social gathering that he needed a math teacher for the upcoming school year, Randy didn't balk at the opportunity.

When he had first received his credentials and went out looking for teaching positions, he made a disappointing discovery: there were no teaching positions. A recession gripped the United States. The American economy had crapped out. So did the prospects for getting into education. With Randy's friend's encouragement and promises, Randy sought the open math position through the proper channels.

Randy Jones had been teaching math at Garza Junior High School for two years, when an incident happened that would change his perceptions of education, fairness, and teaching. It had a marked effect on his life.

On that morning, one of his prized math students walked to the front of his desk. Paul (of Asian ancestry, but with an Anglo first name), timidly said to Mr. Jones, "Sir, I couldn't get my homework done last night. I'm sorry."

Paul clearly had an "A" grade in the class. He was leaps and bounds ahead of the other kids in eighth-grade geometry. Mr. Jones didn't see Paul's problem as a big deal. He shrugged, "That's okay, Paul. Missing one assignment isn't going to hurt your score."

Although Mr. Jones was a tad surprised that Paul *had* missed even one homework assignment, he had told Paul the truth: basically, no harm done.

But as he stood before Mr. Jones, Paul seemed to shrink. Paul was already a small child, short and slight. Culturally, Korean kids tend to get taller than other Asian children. But Paul had not yet begun his ascent. More than before, Paul's words gave Randy the impression he was terrified about something else. Paul said, "Yes, Mr. Jones, Sir. It is going to hurt me. Please let me turn the assignment in late. I have a good reason for not doing it yet."

"Oh, okay," Mr. Jones said. "What happened?" Mr. Jones didn't really care what happened. It wouldn't affect his decision. Paul would be allowed to turn in the work late. This was an easy call.

But Paul cowered. He replied, "I can't tell you what happened."

Now, here is where the story becomes dicey. Mr. Jones knows there is a rule; it is a department rule, a math department rule: no late homework assignments will be accepted, *unless a valid excuse is presented, preferably ahead of time, to the teacher.*

Obviously, Paul's situation did not constitute *ahead of time*. But did he have a valid excuse?

"Honestly," Mr. Jones said later, shaking his head, "I would have accepted *any* excuse from Paul. I didn't even care *what* the excuse was!" He sighed, shook his head again. "This was such a little thing to have.... I don't understand." And then his voice trailed off.

"Oh, okay," Mr. Jones said. "What happened?"

Paul's voice faltered. "I—I can't tell you what happened."

"Well," Mr. Jones shrugged, in hindsight, much too flippantly, "if you can't tell me what happened, then I can't let you turn in your homework later."

"I thought that would be all," Mr. Jones later said. His voice then softened, projecting sadness and confusion. "A child should be able to make a mistake. Isn't that what this is about? But on my end, too: I—we—should allow children, especially children who are well motivated and decent, to make mistakes . . ."

"I can't tell you the reason, Mr. Jones!" Paul repeated. But his voice grew stronger, louder, frantic in its tone. "Can't I just do the assignment and give to you tomorrow? It's not a big deal."

"My point, exactly, Paul," Mr. Jones said. "It's not a big deal. So, just tell me what's—"

"Please, Mr. Jones!"

Paul had begun to sound like a little bit of a nut. His plaintive tone, his wide eyes, begging, pleading. Mr. Jones looked at him squarely, and asked, "So, what happened to your homework?"

"Are you going to let me turn it in?"

"Are you going to tell me why it's not finished?"

"No."

"Then—no," Mr. Jones said, with a firm finality to his voice.

And that was that: at least, Randy Jones *thought* that was that.

Mrs. Medina

The doctors informed Mrs. Medina that she has breast cancer. She might get a mastectomy. She might die. Mrs. Medina has much to think about, to distract her, from teaching her twelfth-grade English class.

The class, though, busily prattles on and on about nothing. They haven't heard about Mrs. Medina's cancer. Mrs. Medina is wondering how she is going to tell her husband of ten years and their seven-year-old daughter. She's not sure if her seven-year-old daughter knows what cancer is.

Mrs. Medina, in her thirties, having taught high school English for ten years, faces the biggest crisis of her life. But she is a professional. She is a teacher. Her various responsibilities, as she views them, extend beyond herself. She will give her husband the frightening news; his world will be rocked. She will allay her daughter's fears, and although those fears will not be concrete, they will be real to the second grader. Even though she won't tell her students about her medical plight—not today—they will soon find out.

The irony is that her students cared the least about her cancer; yet they would ultimately demand most of Mrs. Medina's time and energy. Graduation is looming. The curtain is near. Mrs. Medina has decisions to make.

The humanity of America's teachers never receives much attention. Only incidentally are teachers identified in a positive way, unless the label directly relates to their jobs. ("The academic decathlon's teacher, Mr. Yang, who last week told newspaper reporters how proud he was of his students, died today.")[2]

When you were in elementary school and looked at your teachers in awe, you wanted to be just like them. You wanted to be like them, not because you had a burning desire to impart knowledge and wisdom to a bunch of bratty kids who couldn't control their screechy voices and squiggly limbs; you yearned to have the power and jurisdiction and . . . *esteem* that your own teachers projected. Teachers seemed to have it all together. They seemed to have it all goin' on! They knew so much, hurt so little, and made it perfectly clear *they* were the ones in control.

But how much of that perception was reality? Not by way of *excuses*, but by way of *information*, there are certain *facts* you should know. These facts allow you to understand what teachers go through, what they must deal with in meeting their commitments to their students. The path they take isn't always a straight line, the course painless and trouble free.

1. Teachers die early.

Sorry, that isn't pretty.

Want the bleak truth? A high number of teachers die before they get to retirement age, or before they actually retire, even if they have reached retirement age. Teachers are number one on the list in that dismal regard. They fall (literally) ahead of lawyers and cops. What's interesting about police officers is that the average age of retirement is 57; for teachers it is 61. Teachers have a harder time reaching their retirement age than do police officers. Weirdly, *doctors* die early, too, but teachers beat doctors to the grave, as well. It isn't as bad as it is for those coal miners, but still . . .

On average, teachers live about 2.6 years after they retire, no matter what their retirement age. That's the average. So a teacher who retires at age 57 and dies at 58 is figured in with those who retire at age 62 and die at 85. A lot of teachers are not making it very far into retirement.[3]

Factors for premature deaths among teachers during their retirement:

- The wear and tear of the job
- Depression after retiring from the job
- Boredom
- Fatigue
- Sudden change in lifestyle and exercise patterns
- Medical effects brought on by stress
- Poor diet and health habits (including alcoholism: a high percentage of teachers tend to be drunks)
- The shock of having to spend an inordinate amount of time with spouses

Who knows how many teachers dwell on these statistics while they are approaching retirement, but no matter: teachers have it rough. The job takes its toll a lot more than people outside the profession are aware.

2. *Teachers are not financially secure.*

Although teachers in most states have relatively sound retirement programs, they are prohibited from taking out their retirement money, even to use for emergencies. It's not like a 401K.

Projections on retirement earnings tell us that for a teacher to arrive at a place where his retirement earnings would provide a little financial security, he would have to have taught for at least twenty-five consecutive years; he would not be sitting on the lower rungs of the salary schedule ladder.

A majority of school districts in America do not provide life insurance policies, and among those that do provide policies, they are rarely worth more than twenty or thirty thousand dollars. The difficulty for teachers to acquire adequate life insurance can't be overstated. Teachers have health issues. Remember, teachers die early. Not very many companies will insure a forty-five-year-old man or woman who has a blood pressure reading of 175 or has a cholesterol level of 200.

Few school districts in the United States provide medical benefits for teachers and their dependents while they are retired. Some districts will, but just a few. After teachers die, their dependents are cut off. Retired teachers must purchase medical insurance, just like the rest of the poor schmucks in the population. And that can, for a family of four, run upward of six or seven hundred dollars a month—*at group rates*. Regular rates can cost a family of four around $2,000 a month! That is quite a drain on a retired teacher's monthly retirement check.[4]

3. *Teachers divorce.*

The strain from having a broken family is enormous. Teachers' divorce rates are not as high as those of police officers or lawyers, but they are up there. As divorce statistics show, there are numerous reasons for this phenomenon. But stress, financial problems, and time taken away from family all contribute to ugly divorce rates.

Divorced teacher Ty Grimsley said,[5] "My ex-wife told me that when I came home from work it was like I was still in my classroom, ordering around the kids and her. I used too loud a voice and felt like I always needed to be in control of everything.... When I felt like I was losing that control, I was a son-of-a-bitch to be around."

Thank you, Ty, for an honest appraisal of your disposition to which many can easily relate.

4. Teachers never leave their job sites.

Mostly because they take their job sites home with them.

Amazingly, the public criticizes teachers for having summers off (for which they do not get paid) and holidays to spend with families. But most of today's teachers will tell you this is not the case: they are working practically all the time! In fact, considering the amount of time they are planning, teaching, attending extra school-related activities, and grading and assessing students, teachers earn less than the hourly minimum wage![6]

The teaching profession falls into three major areas of construct: actual teaching, which includes meetings, reporting to parents, and handling difficult situations for which there may be conferences and other emergency meetings; preparation, which includes research, conferences, and hardcore lesson planning; and assessment, which includes grading papers, tests, and figuring grades for parental feedback, notifications, and report cards.

Computers make most jobs more accessible at home; the same goes for teaching. But the work lingers; it festers. It doesn't go away. Those who ignore their work or put it off until later, still have to do it . . . sometime. If they don't, they are bad teachers. And they start to grow puss on their upper lip.[7]

People know who the bad teachers are. Teachers know who the bad teachers are. Even bad teachers know who the other bad teachers are. And most teachers do not want to fall into the category of bad teacher.[8]

5. Teachers and parents are deceptively divided.

You might think that being a teacher and being a parent are somewhat close on the topography map. The general public thinks it is so. Teachers, before they became teachers, thought it was so: *Myrna has no children. She has been a kindergarten teacher for twelve years and has never had any children of her own. Too bad. She would have been a great mother!*

Or . . .

I understand teenagers. I do. I've taught high school for ten years. It's about time I had children. When they become teenagers, I will be a fantastic father!

Or sometimes you hear this one:

I am almost fifty. I've taught elementary school for over twenty-five years. I never got married and had kids because I didn't have the time. I was always distracted by my job. Who had time to socialize? Who had time to date? Who had time to find the right man to have children with? Not me. But I guess the good part is . . . well, I've had children for twenty-five years. I've had hundreds of children!

With all due respect, being a fourth-grade teacher to a classroom of kids and mothering children of your own are not the same thing. To truly understand this, you would have to be both a mother *and* a teacher. They are different. They are both incredibly difficult. They are both tremendously rewarding. But they are different. If you had been both, you would totally get it.

So, why bring this up? What's the point?

Ironically, children with parents who are also teachers often find themselves uncomfortable attending school. Most kids hang around in groups of friends where their discussions about their teachers do not cast those teachers in a favorable light. Far from it. Finding out your friend's mother teaches eighth grade is like finding out your friend's mother is a pole dancer at Louden's Bar—only worse, because at least the pole dancer brings joy to a lot of people and doesn't threaten to ruin a kid's life by filling out a report card that could result in parent-induced starvation or involuntary servitude. Cases of withholding this kind of information from friends are abundant. They often sound something like this:

> *So, what is it that your father does for a living?*
> *I'm not sure.*
> *I heard he's an English teacher at some high school.*
> *Nah. Where did you hear that?*
> *I—*
> *He's not an English teacher. He's the varsity football coach.*
> *Really? Cool! How long has he been coaching?*
> *Shut up!*

God help the kid who attends a school where one of his parents is a teacher! Jeez! How awful would that be! You would have to possess the fortitude to hear what a jerk or dimwit or idiot or weirdo your father is! Even if you agree your father is one of these things—or all of them—listening to it said repeatedly by your peers has to be hard to take. Somewhere along the line, you would be tempted to pack your suitcase and head for the hills. There might not be any hills, but you would scurry somewhere, anywhere, just to escape the unpleasant verbiage strewn toward your father—or mother—and sometimes you.

Your only crime: being the son or daughter of a teacher at your own school.

Parents who are teachers suddenly discover—maybe they *slowly* discover—that their parenting paths and their teacher paths are sometimes opposites, often in conflict. The hardness, the objectivity they must hold as teachers, is softened because they are parents, too. They see other peoples' children in a more subjective light. After all, that girl who has come late to school five days in a row could have been their daughter, the one they fight tooth and nail every morning just to get her out of bed and to school on time, without any degree of success.

The teaching profession develops a slightly different set of conditions for dealing with these kinds of issues. Students', parents', and the publics' *perceptions* of teachers, in large part, account for a teacher's anointment of success. Hardly anyone looks at one of her teachers and thinks about that teacher getting sick or having marital problems. That isn't supposed to happen.

A teacher is a rock, a pillar, a guiding light; she is not an alcoholic, a woman who sneaks a bottle of vodka into her classroom and hides it in her desk drawer, while taking the occasional sip throughout the school day, only because she is too weak to wait until she gets home, where she can bury her classroom sorrows, while binge watching *Breaking Bad*.

Mr. Jones

Back to math teacher Mr. Jones, who denied an intense young student, Paul, a request to turn in a homework assignment a day late: Paul refused to reveal to Mr. Jones the reason his assignment would be late, which was part of the conditions for Mr. Jones to grant Paul an extension of time. Paul seemed frantic about the situation, but did not budge from his mum-is-the-word position; neither did Mr. Jones alter his stance.

Most jobs have certain hazards attached. Firefighters run into burning buildings and can die instantly. Miners deal with lung problems. Doctors keep long, odd hours and must be ready at a moment's notice to ride to the rescue of a patient, sometimes forfeiting vacation time and special moments with their families.

Teachers are often thrust into decision-making scenarios that result in enormous ramifications they may not have foreseen. Sometimes those decisions have to do with assigning a grade that determines a student's graduation status; other times, a teacher's decision affects a student's social status (as in nixed from attending the senior prom); and infrequent moments of misinformed decision making can lead to consequences the teacher could not have foretold because the reaction of those on the other end was unreasonable, a non sequitur, seemingly unrelated to the significance of the circumstances and the severity of the consequences.

Paul's suicide may have been related to factors that had nothing to do with his schooling, his education, or his plans for his future. No one will ever know for sure what he was thinking that night, when he removed the gun from an old dresser his father kept in his tool supply closet. He clearly intended to end his young life; that was clear to investigators.

His friends related to the police Paul's consternation over the missing homework incident in Mr. Jones's math class. His parents doubled down on the homework theory. Paul's mother, in a tearful rant, told the police that Mr. Jones had stubbornly refused to allow her son to turn in his homework. He had never missed an assignment—in *any* class. Certainly, an exception to such a stringent policy could have been made in the case of a student like Paul.

The bantering over this tragedy borders on the ludicrous. Mr. Jones said later, "I would have given him full credit for the assignment if he would have followed policy by letting me know why he did not have his homework with him that morning. He could have lied. He could have told me anything. In the case of Paul, I would have been okay with it. Besides . . . that we are even talking about the homework assignment right now is rather peculiar, isn't it?"[9]

Especially because of the *facts* that emerged in the months that followed:

- Paul had been saturated with Paxil. His psychological condition had been impaired.[10]
- Paul's therapist later told of Paul's talk of suicide. *Before the fact*, he had also expressed his grave concerns to Paul's parents.
- Paul's parents had been putting inordinate pressure on their son to succeed in school. Success was measured by his grades. "Success" could mean only straight-A grades. Success was measured by his intelligence, his cut above the rest of the flock when it came to being smart, precise, and keen about his subject grades.
- Paul did not do his math homework because he did not understand it. He could not tell this to his parents. He could not confess his "weakness" to his teacher. Paul's math tutor was scheduled to work with Paul the fateful afternoon of his death. As usual, his tutor would help him to understand, make his homework an easy task. It would bring him to a place of understanding with the math concepts he previously had not comprehended. Mr. Jones would take his assignment one day late. It would be all right.

"He could have said to me, 'My tutor is coming this afternoon and will help me with the work. Once I understand it, I will do it.' I would have been fine with that," Mr. Jones said later, shaking his head, wistfully looking about the room. "This whole thing . . . what a shame. What a lousy shame. Just thinking about it . . . it doesn't make any sense. How can a kid be so afraid of his parents, so ashamed, that he would end his life over not turning an insignificant math worksheet?"

Nobody blamed Mr. Jones for what happened to Paul. Even Paul's parents, after their initial shock and grief, backed off from doing that. Paul's psychologist placed no blame, either. But the culture of success at any cost, the shame of failure, the pressure of parenting . . . all contributed to a scene that could have easily been avoided.

Or *could* it have been avoided?

Paul's psychologist didn't think so. "I told Paul's parents of my concerns, my belief that he should seek further counseling. I wrote them referrals. It wasn't a lone homework incident that led to this. Paul was racked with pressures he couldn't handle. He was cumulatively affected by the strains in his life. He saw his schooling as what defined him. His parents saw Paul's grades as what defined *them*."[11]

And maybe what defines everybody here: *crazy*.

Mr. Jones, almost four years after Paul's death, has not fully recovered—not even close. Intellectually, he knows he did not drive Paul to suicide. But emotionally, he can't separate from the idea that it would have been so easy for him to wave his hand at Paul and let him off the hook. Given Paul's high scores in his class, his conscientiousness, having not done the relatively insignificant homework didn't matter.

Yet he believes that Paul, if not propelled by this minor incident—given his psychological condition—would have eventually wound up in the same place. As a classroom teacher, Mr. Jones had become the unlucky recipient of being in the wrong place at the wrong time.

Mr. Jones's story is anecdotal. By no means does it denote what all classroom teachers in America face. On a smaller emotional scale, though, teachers are required to make decisions and deal with conditions that are not found in "How To Be A Teacher" primers.[12] Like so many on-the-job learning experiences found in other professions, there can be no turning back the hands of time once the dye has been cast.

Mrs. Medina

Mrs. Medina did nothing to bring on her cancer. She made no decisions, gave no advice. She wound up with cancer because . . . she did.

Through no fault of her own, she simultaneously had to raise two children and attend to a job that provided medical insurance. That insurance would provide her only hope of recovery and normalcy. Teaching, though, was not an ordinary job. The demands and pressures knew no mercy. Her students were nearing the end of their long journey toward their high school graduation, and any pity or empathy they extended toward their teacher was purely coincidental.

One of the perks of retirement is that a former teacher has the newfound opportunity to go to the bathroom whenever she wants.

Bathroom luxuries come in handy as people age. By the time they reach retirement, they *have* aged. Teachers spend their days timing their bathroom breaks, scheduling them around other activities, such as meetings with parents, running the copy machine in the teachers lounge, and eating lunch. Demanding schedules require teachers to stay away from personal bathroom functions for three, four consecutive hours or more! At that, bathrooms on campus open up for a limited time, becoming crowded and embarrassing to use.

Teachers face high incidences of constipation, diarrhea, Crohn's disease, diverticulitis, and irritable bowel syndrome, along with that occasional urge to run into the bathroom and throw water on their faces.

Teaching pegs *itself* as the profession that doesn't stop for an emergency dump. It can't. If a man is teaching in a third-grade classroom, he can't all of a sudden excuse himself and hightail it to the toilet. By the time he has alerted the security guard to his embarrassing crisis, he may have already gone to the point of no return. Teachers have reoccurring nightmares about such states of affairs.

Another emergency situation: not one in which the teacher has to change his underwear; he may have to change his bandages, however. All teachers, especially those on a middle school or high school campus have been thrust into the unenviable position of having to break up a fight between a couple of kids.

Mr. Pasternik innocently sat in his classroom eating a ham sandwich during his lunch break. He heard commotion outside and decided to ignore it. He initially thought it didn't require an immediate response. But the noise, a loud rumbling sound, accompanied by the excited shouts of teenagers, grew louder.

The combatants in the fight spilled through his open classroom door. They knocked over a desk near the entrance. The classroom was empty, so Mr. Pasternik could move swiftly through the room. He glimpsed the boys and assessed that they were larger than he was.

His teacher instincts took over. He grabbed one of the kids around his waist, from behind. Because the other boy was angrily charging toward the restrained pugilist, Mr. Pasternik feared for the safety of the boy he had been holding back. He pulled him, hard, and fell backward in the process. Mr. Pasternik, boy in tow, slammed his back into a few desks before he hit the floor, his arms still wrapped around the kid. It may have looked brutal, but the teacher's hold of the youngster protected the kid and broke up the fight.

Both students were suspended. The onlookers had a thrill. Mr. Pasternik wound up with a bruised shoulder. He later recounted that he didn't realize he had hit his shoulder on the desk on his way down to the floor. He was so intensely aware of his duty to protect the boys from each other that his own needs took second priority to those of the combatants.

Nothing heroic here. Nothing out of the ordinary. It just goes with the territory. A teacher is thrust into unpleasant emergency duty and he doesn't think about the particulars of what he is doing. He simply knows it has to be done. He is injured, and for that, he will receive some—not much—sympathy from staff members at the school.

Next time it might be worse. Next time there could be a shooter on campus. Which is what happened in Sparks, Nevada, when Mike Landberry was shot and killed in the school's cafeteria by a student who began firing at other students during their lunch break. The run-astray kid, without apparent motive or warning, had shot two other boys before Mr. Landberry tried to intervene—and the teacher lost his own life in the process.[13]

Other frightening episodes have dotted the headlines. A teacher was murdered at Columbine High School during the infamous attack in Littleton, Colorado, where twenty-one kids lost their lives. Business teacher, forty-eight-year-old William David Sanders, was gunned down by one of the two creeps that attacked the suburban school, in April 1999.[14]

Teacher Victoria Soto gave her own life in New Town, Connecticut, after saving her first-grade students by hiding them in a closet at Sandy Hook Elementary School, where twenty-one little kids died in 2013.[15]

Teachers can't run and hide. They must be on the front lines, no matter what. Other peoples' children are entrusted to them; it is the teacher's obligation to protect those children.[16] Like police officers, teachers do not think twice about jumping into action, and when they die—far more rarely than it happens to cops—other people accurately assume it is an unfortunate part of their job description.[17]

Mr. Jones continues to teach high school mathematics. He has not been the same since the tragedy that touched him so deeply. He doesn't blame himself for the death of his student, but he is dumbfounded by the trivial nature of the events that perpetuated it. And he lives with bitter anger.

Mrs. Medina continues to teach high school English. She lost a breast during her fight against cancer, but she did not become a casualty. Her own perspective about what matters in life has changed drastically. When her students tell her there are people and events that are more important than making up a quiz they did poorly on, Mrs. Medina understands them, for she knows there *are* things much more important than that quiz.

Teachers must know their goals and their motivations: applying the test of perspective to the adversity that you face every day; understanding where others are coming from after they have studied your reputation and what you are about; realizing that no matter what other people may think, *you* are important; and *as long as you do the right thing, you will be able to live with yourself.*

These attitudes: they are survival skills for a world that makes the life of a teacher more difficult than it should be.

NOTES

1. Amy Rosmarin, "Parents Need to Be Reminded That Teachers Are People Too," *Thought Catalogue*, October 16, 2013, http://thoughtcatalog.com/abby-rosmarin/2013/10/par-

ents-need-to-be-reminded-that-teachers-are-people-too/. I figured a brash declarative sentence such as this needed to be supported by at least one other source.

2. Around 95 percent of the people who read the news story about Mr. Yang thought to themselves, "Who's *that* guy? What's *he* do?"

3. Michael Lai, "Early Retirement=Early Death?" *Retireediary*, April 17, 2012, https://retireediary.wordpress.com/2012/04/17/early-retirement-early-death/. The answer is . . . yes.

4. The retiree, who collects a monthly check of around $4,800, must figure out a way to continue his health coverage. Obviously, a monthly $2,000 is out of the question so he searches for other ways to provide. Any ideas? (Oh, do not retire. Is that an option?)

5. "The Reasons Why Sir Goes Extra-Curricular," *Times Higher Education*, October 6, 2000, https://www.timeshighereducation.com/news/the-reason-why-sir-goes-extracurricular/153775.article. Teachers do not come even close to bartenders and dance choreographers in divorce rates, however.

6. When teaching hours, time spent going to meetings, workshops, and in-services, grading papers, doing lesson plans, and shopping for teaching materials are figured into the salary equation, a beginning teacher earns about ten dollars an hour, give or take a few bucks.

7. Yup.

8. The only label that is worse: *bad writer*.

9. Alfie Kohn, *The Homework Myth* (Cambridge, MA: Da Capo Press, 2006). A principal makes a powerful case against homework. The psychological and physiological effects he cites are staggering. Much of this book reads like a medical journal.

10. "Best Depression Device," http://www.drugs.com/paxil.html. Paxil is a strong antidepressant medication that is not recommended for anyone under eighteen years of age without the okay from a doctor. One of its side effects: it may help to induce thoughts of suicide.

11. Parents who do this should rip up their parenting card. To define your child by what kind of grades she gets in school is a despicable self-centeredness and self-absorption that defies the imagination of decent people. These people are clearly all about the *parent* and not at all about the child.

12. "A First Year Teacher's Primer," *Education World*, May 22, 2016, http://www.educationworld.com/first-year-teachers-primer. Here is an actual example of one of those primers! Go figure.

13. Catherine E. Shoichet, Amanda Watts, and Chuck Johnston, "Teacher Killed, Two Students Wounded," CNN, October 21, 2013, http://www.cnn.com/2013/10/21/justice/nevada-middle-school-shooting/.

14. James Barron, "Terror in Littleton: The Dead," *New York Times*, April 23, 1999, Part I, 1.

15. Sara Hammel and Mike Freeman, "Hero Teacher Dies Saving Students," *People*, December 15, 2012, http://www.people.com/people/package/article/0,,20656736_20657003,00.html.

16. Sandy Hook, Columbine, Sparks: let those be metaphors for a teacher's responsibility. Rarely does exercising responsibility happen unto death, but almost every teacher I know would have done the same thing under similar circumstances.

17. Few teachers have laid down their physical lives for their students—at least, directly; however, there have been numerous cases of teachers actually killing their students with boredom. That needs to be worked on, too.

Chapter Eleven

The Naked Emperor

The veteran teacher stood in the corridor of his school district's main office building. He felt his knees shaking; beads of moisture sat poised, ready to roll off his forehead. *I'm not going back in there!,* he thought to himself, as he let his back slide against the wall behind him. *I can't take this anymore!*

Shannon Bateman followed the teacher into the corridor. About ten years older than Mr. Kenson, the teacher against the corridor wall, Mrs. Bateman was the science department chairperson at the high school where the two had taught for a combined fifty-four years. Mrs. Bateman felt an urgency to quell her colleague's anger before he wound up doing something he would regret.

Jack Kenson was one of the most popular teachers on campus, a highly touted science instructor. He received national recognition for his articles, published in various well-known journals. He had an air of confidence about him, to the point where that confidence threatened to bleed into arrogance.

At the district-wide symposium on standardized testing, the subject of SAT scores arose. The presenter, fully equipped to lambast high school educators because of the scores, went further than anyone in the room had anticipated. She presented a cultural and racial breakdown of SAT results from the previous year: at the bottom of the list, were the scores of black and Hispanic children.

Jack politely raised his hand and asked the presenter, "What does that mean?"

The presenter chuckled knowingly, a smug snicker. She said, "It means we're not doing a good enough job teaching children from those groups."

"Why is that?" Jack asked, his eyebrows raised.

"Good question. It's an important question to ask," the presenter nodded, suddenly sounding not as condescending, but a little more patronizing.

Jack persisted. "Are you saying that teachers in the public schools are racist? That's the main reason why scores from those groups of kids are so low?"

Every educator in the room carefully watched the presenter, as she poised herself to answer Jack's question. Nobody, including Jack, had expected her answer. She looked dolefully around the room and shrugged. She said, "Sometimes when we ask questions like that, we have to prepare for the truth, even if it's not to our liking."

"Then you *are* saying we're racists," Jack accused.

The presenter looked at those in the room, deferred to Jack, and spread her hands. It was a nonverbal *if the shoe fits, wear it* implication.

Which infuriated Jack, who rose from his seat and stormed, "Well, I really don't have to listen to any more of this shit!" before scurrying from the room and into the corridor, where Shannon Bateman, the department chairperson, worked to pacify him.

Shannon explained to Jack that many in society possessed similar concerns to those being voiced by the presenter. Jack and the others in the room were expected to listen to her, make comments, and then go on their merry ways—most of them back to their schools, where they do a tremendous job with all students of all races, despite the problems implicit in the SAT scores.

But Jack would have none of that. He made it his goal to research those scores and to figure out the real reasons minority children did not compete well with Caucasian and Asian children when it came to SATs.

Waiting for Superman deals mostly with minority children. Problems inherent in their neighborhoods have pilfered the education of these children. They are falling further and further behind. The SAT scores are merely the tip of the iceberg.

The truth is that *teachers are not to blame for the special challenges minority children face in public education.*

That should be stated again: The truth is that *teachers are not to blame for the special challenges minority children face in public education.*

The following *are* truths about our schools and minority students. Before checking into how America's teachers figure into this, clarifying the facts is in order:

1. American schools in mostly minority neighborhoods stink.
2. Schools in minority neighborhoods stink, but these problems do not stem from regional poverty.
3. These problems do not stem from teacher inadequacies.
4. These problems do not stem from systematic racism or cultural biases.
5. Minorities in schools populated by mostly white and/or Asian students tend to do less effectively in their studies than whites and Asians.

A breakdown of the problems faced by blacks and Hispanics in American schools shows that students fall into one of two categories: (1) those minority students who are attending schools *not* in minority neighborhoods and (2) those students, including Caucasian and Asian students, who are attending schools in mostly minority neighborhoods.[1]

Veering from an endnote to a text reference, just in case you did not see the footnote: Asian students are not counted as minorities in America—at least when it comes to our public schools, colleges and universities, and most other aspects of American life, including prisons. Even though Koreans, Japanese, Chinese, and Pacific Islanders make up only 6 percent of America's schoolchildren,[2] these children are given their own classification: *Asian*. Not majority or minority—just *Asian*. And check this out: children who are fifty-fifty, half Asian (Korean, for example) and half something else, are classified as Korean, not the something else. So a kid might be 40 percent Korean and 60 percent Mexican; he is still considered Korean and, thus, not a minority student.

When there are more than two cultures or races in the mix, or when the percentage of Asian drops, and something else rises, it gets a little peculiar. In fact, figuring this out in the first place—a percentage of blood and racial mixtures—is rather odd!

TRUTH: American schools in mostly minority neighborhoods stink. That truth is as plain as the nose on Ted Cruz's face. An abundance of evidence supports this claim. Most people do not require being hit over the head with information about how terrible schools are in the inner city. They already know. Hearing about it makes them sick. What they purport to want are *solutions* to those problems.

But for refreshment, Oscar Alan Singer, of the Huffington Post, wrote, "Students enter buildings through metal detectors. Armed police stand guard. Uniformed security crews that report to the police sweep the halls. Students are forced to sit in overcrowded uncomfortable classrooms doing rote assignments geared to high-stakes Common Core assessments. Stressed out teachers, fearful that they will be judged by poor student performance on these tests, use boredom and humiliation to maintain control of the classroom."[3]

TRUTH: Schools in mostly minority neighborhoods stink, but the problems do not stem from poverty.

What?

Isn't poverty the cause of hunger, crime, inflation, and almost every ailment out there? Come on! The poorer people are, the worse they tend to do in life. And that's just a plain *fact*, right?

Hmm . . .

Think again:

Fatherlessness breeds domestic strife . . .

Domestic strife breeds poverty . . .

BUT what makes the schools so crappy? Domestic strife or poverty?

The lack of money breeds poverty, right? That's the same as saying a lack of food breeds starvation.

Duh!

But what causes the lack of food? You figure that out, and you don't have hunger. You figure out what causes *conditions* that lead to poverty and solve *that* problem, then you don't have underdeveloped, unfunded, unorganized, ineffectual schools in mostly minority neighborhoods. But it's not a lack of money that causes kids' schooling problems. Nope. Think again.

There is one commonality for the above problems: fatherlessness. For seventy years or so, sociologists have lamented on the poverty of the inner city. The cries, far and wide, were for more money (in the form of welfare payments) to women. Without a dad in the home, there is only one income. Boys, especially, are likely to commit crimes, violent ones. Without a dad in the house, boys are much more likely to wind up in prison.[4]

The connection between poverty and crime is tenuous. The connection between fatherlessness and crime is *not* tenuous; it is *stark*. Sociologists like to leap over the middle connection pole in order to arrive at their preordained conclusions. Boys do not commit crimes because they are poor; they commit crimes because they are unsupervised, run wild, lack values, and have no fear. The threatening voice of, "Wait 'til your father gets home!" has been replaced by, "Can't wait 'til the welfare check arrives in the mail!"

Fatherlessness leads to a whole host of problems; one of them is poverty. Even in affluent families where the father is dead, or the father has abandoned his wife and kids, or he and the mother have divorced, juvenile delinquency rates soar.

In poor neighborhoods, the kids don't leap out of bed in the morning with a big smile on their faces and rush off to school while singing "Oh, What a Beautiful Morning!"

America's teachers are human beings—smart, educated, and talented. They can't be expected to pull off miracles, although some do. Those that do tend to make other teachers look bad.

Teachers require some luck, too. Luck only comes once in a while. They can't rely on luck. Here are eight crucial observations about the destruction of inner city schools, not suburban schools, not rural schools—*inner city schools*. These schools make the rest look like royal castles. They make learning that goes on in these schools apropos to Harvard University.

"Where does your kid go to school, Mrs. Miller?"

"Harvard."

"Harvard? Isn't he still in high school?"

"Yeah, but I know, but compared to where your kids go to school, my kid's school *is Harvard.*"

That has to change. Teachers are not to blame for ghetto schools. They can only do so much to fix them, too. Here are eight crucial concepts to consider.

1. America's schools are sectionalized.

That is the nature of the beast. Pockets of poverty breed their own neighborhood schools. Those schools receive just as much money—sometimes more—from their respective states than the pretty rich, all-white schools. The federal government coughs up the bucks, too. But blacks and Hispanics tend to live in segregated neighborhoods. These neighborhoods are not segregated by law; they aren't even segregated by conscious efforts to segregate them. They just are what they are, for a multitude of reasons.

These places are commonly referred to as *the Ghetto*.

In some areas of the country, Jews have their self-styled "ghetto." And everybody has heard of Korea Town and Chinatown and the like. People like to be around their own. They like to confide and confer with their own. "Their own" is often determined by criteria having to do with skin color, national origin, and culture.

America's educators must deal with this sectionalism. Going into these tough neighborhoods and trying to teach school is not usually at the top of anyone's list of things to do, especially for teachers coming out of graduate schools. But someone has to do it. If that is where the jobs are, that is where the jobs are.[5]

2. Teachers prefer to stay away from inner city schools.

Who wants to go *there*? The crime rate has gone up faster in these places than the point totals of teams that play the Los Angeles Lakers. Children are tougher to teach, and they miss an inordinate number of days of school. When the children at these schools do not learn—and the norm is, unfortunately, that they do not learn much—teachers catch hell: for not being able to teach them; for being too soft on discipline; for dealing with students in ways that broadcast weak and defensive policies and personalities.

The salaries teachers receive for working in these schools are rarely any higher than the salaries teachers receive for working at other schools, those in safer, preferable neighborhoods. Some teachers volunteer to go to the slum schools because they figure this is the only way they can hang on to their jobs; others go there because they have been sent, sometimes against their will. And some teachers work at the inner city school because they consider it their calling. They believe it is what they have been meant to do ever since they entered the teaching profession, maybe even before that, during the time they worked part-time at the local bowling alley.

3. *A disproportionate number of students at these schools are using or selling drugs.*

What did he say?

What?

It is not a secret. Sure, drugs are all around us, mired particularly deep in the youth culture of America. But fatherlessness makes way for the influx of valueless souls. Children feel disconnected. They envy other kids whose parents actively participate in their lives and encourage them to succeed. They become void of feelings, withdrawing into an abyss of indifference. Sometimes they percolate into anger, a fury brought about by that perpetual indifference; and they seek attention in almost any way they can get it.

That attention seeking takes on many forms, not all of them positive. Drugs wiggle their way into these children's lives, sometimes at the unripe age of impressionability. It's easy to see how conniving adults befriend ten-year-old kids, manipulating them into lives of drug abuse and prostitution.

The children who live in sequestered communities, cut off because of economic deprivation and criminal activity, attend schools that inherit their ills. Society assigns teachers the task of taking care of these children, and if ever there was a place in which a teacher must carry the multiple burdens of teacher, counselor, doctor, and cop, these schools are that place.

Boston teacher Rooney Ratzfield may have summarized a lot of teacher's frustrations, when he said, "It gets so bad, I hope my students *don't* show up for classes. . . . That's the bad part and the good part. Of course, it's better when students come to school. But . . . it's also better when they don't."[6]

4. *Attendance is erratic.*

Children who grow up largely unsupervised have a great deal more latitude on whether they make it out the front door in the morning and arrive at school. Most American school kids are either awakened by a parent or by their cell phone alarms. But in these economically and socially deprived sectors of the country, the structure to enforce such disciplines is nonexistent. If a child hates school, as most children do, she simply does not go to school that day . . . or week or month.

If a child has an impulsive desire to do something else, say burglarize homes, he does so. No one is there to stop him. If a child can't get up in the morning because he has been out drinking—or doing drugs or gang banging—all night, he may lie in bed comatose. No one is there to badger him from his bed, out the door, and to school.

School attendance in these neighborhoods is disastrous.[7]

The upshot of this difficult problem is twofold: (1) schools lose revenue (Americans with Disabilities Act money) and (2) students don't learn (they are not in school). The long-range upshot could be tragic, the economic consequences disastrous. We've seen it already happen. The horrific aftermath in the education community is that *teachers* are blamed for these problems. Kids don't come to class. Kids don't learn because they are not in school: it's racism. It *has* to be racism. If not within the education establishment itself, it's all over the place.

Because of racism, children don't come to school.

Maybe that sounded a tad sarcastic.

5. *Parental support is . . . what parental support?*

Cedrick Wegmeyer, an assistant principal at a school in East Los Angeles—a well-known school—made a comment recorded here in its exact context. Tempted to censor or alter his remarks, your humble author decided not to. Ultimately, people have to know what educators are dealing with. At the very least, educators should provide the public, parents, and political leadership their take on barriers to achieving the kinds of results that would satisfy the masses. Educators haven't come close to satisfying the masses, or even placating the few; that is why words such as these should be heard in their entirety:

> Last week, one of our security guards found a ten-year-old boy, a fourth grader, hiding in a bathroom during our lunch period. She [the security guard] found him in one of the stalls with the door locked. After coaxing him out of the stall, she brought him to my office, where I found out a few things. The boy—we'll call him Chris—was hungry, had no lunch money, and wasn't signed up for the free lunch program at our school. The free lunch program is pretty generous; all it requires is a parent to sign up the child. But that's where the problem was. His parents never signed him up. In fact, I called his mother's phone, which was in our records as her home phone number, and never got an answer, not even an answering machine. I asked Chris how he usually gets to school, and he said he walks; his mother usually picks him up. But not always. Sometimes he has to walk [the three blocks on city streets] home from school, too. Chris sat in my office for the rest of the afternoon. We gave him a lunch from the cafeteria, which he gobbled up in seconds. His mother didn't show after school, and Chris asked if he could walk home. I told him no. We would have to reach his mother first. Which never happened. I finally dialed the emergency phone number on his registration card, and talked with his maternal grandmother. She came and got the poor kid. Chris's father was never in his life. His young mother, probably not even twenty-five years old herself, spent her days cleaning houses and catering to her drug habit. . . . This was a case of neglect, pure and simple. But, sad to say, it's not the only case like this at our school. African-American and Latino families in our neighborhood don't prioritize the education of their children. It's almost like—am I allowed to say this?—they don't see educating their kids as important as their daily rigors of life. Life is very tough for these people. . . . Their children suffer. Raising kids is hard enough when you have two parents working together. One parent, no real job . . . that's rough. The kids suffer. They suffer all

the time. They don't get educated. They can't find jobs after they get out of high school, *if* they do get out of high school. And our school—it suffers, too. The teachers have a hard time teaching. They must try to contain a bunch of unruly children who have no support at home, no discipline, no rules. Many of them are out gang banging until the wee hours of the morning and then wind up sitting blurry eyed in my classroom a few hours later. Now, ask the teacher to save them. It's not fair. Parental support comes in many forms: working with their children on their studies, encouraging them to succeed, and providing a home life that is conducive to becoming decent, respectful citizens.

In a nutshell, parents must be in the trenches with their kids, manipulating the odds in their children's favor. But that isn't happening. It is worse, far worse, in inner city neighborhoods. Some of the rural sections of the country aren't so terrific either. But this chapter is focusing on schools that get the short end of the socioeconomic stick. Society blames teachers for their failures. They wait for Superman. And when he doesn't come, their anger resonates on the entirety of the teaching profession.

6. *These schools wallow in America's slums.*

I'm sorry, what did he say?
 Did he say these schools wallow in America's slums?
 How dare he say that! There he goes again!

These schools fail. Not all schools that fail sit in the center of a neighborhood that invites poverty and fatherlessness to every doorstep. But the statistics on this matter don't lie. They tell a tale we have already heard, that we already know too well.

Low-cost housing, high-rent housing, overpriced housing, and crowded housing tell the story. Families (often more than one family) that squeeze into rooms built for only one or two people clamor for help, but that help rarely comes. Government subsidies can only go so far. Hunger and crime dominate the landscape. The homeless populate the community, dotting the roadside for too many miles with too few bathrooms.

People should not be surprised to see schools that have taken on the characteristics of their communities. Psychological factors come into play. When a kid leaves his (whatever he calls) home with an empty stomach, in tattered clothing, with groggy eyes from the stresses of family upheaval, his adaptation to school takes on similar proportions. A classroom in the dingy quarters of a school that sits across the street from the bonfires of the homeless and the dumpy dwellings of the economically battered looks and smells and feels like a classroom in hell.

Interestingly, students complain about their predicaments even in schools that are free from these horrid conditions. Parents should say to those privileged kids, "You don't know what a bad school is like. You should see some of the schools! You should *be* in one of those schools! You don't have any idea how lucky you are!"[8]

7. Objectively speaking, these schools reek.

Objectivity in judging America's schools comes from test scores. Other standards of judgment may include graduation rates, early-dropout statistics, crime reports, and expulsion and suspension numbers. More subjective criteria for judging the quality of a school could include extracurricular activities, athletic programs, and the range of courses offered to students.

Schools could also be judged by the licensing requirements met by their teachers, the duration of their teachers at the school, or even their teachers' education levels.

There are dozens of ways to go about judging the quality of a school. Most of them are subjective, as these comments suggest:

- *I love my daughter's elementary school. The teachers there are so nice.*
- *My son's school offers a sports program for sixth graders. Great school.*
- *I like how my daughter's middle school includes the ninth grade; this gets her ready for high school.*
- *My son's school is academically superior to any other school around. It offers four foreign languages as electives.*
- *Westside is the best school in the district. They won CIF (football) two years in a row.*
- *I love the architecture at my kids' school. It's antique. I wish I had gone there.*
- *Brookdale Middle School is a terrible school. The kids have to take three years of P.E.!*
- *My son is in a bad school, in a bad neighborhood. I worry about his safety.*
- *The food here is terrible. The cafeteria needs to serve tacos.*
- *The teachers here are too hard. I hate this school!*
- *I want my children to attend Wakefield Elementary. There are places for drop off and pick up and plenty of parking.*
- *This awful place doesn't have any air conditioning. Horrible school.*
- *I would never send my children to that [elementary] school. The school is not completely fenced in.*
- *The teachers there (at that school) are a bunch of racists. Bad place. Bad school.*

Objectively, or as objective as one can get about judging schools, test scores reign. What's more, when tests are good, schools are good—and homes are even better: their values go up. Obviously, the converse is true.

When a school comes in with lousy test scores, the schools are considered lousy, and home values go down. Hardly anyone wants to buy a home in a neighborhood with poor schools. Unless the homes come dirt cheap. And that's what happens: dirt-cheap homes, based on students in subpar schools performing pitifully on standardized tests. (See chapter 5 for more disappointing reality checks concerning testing trendiness in America's schools.)

Grim reality check: America's schools in the inner cities and rural communities that sit somewhere in the nation's boondocks underperform. Check that: in order to underperform, one must expect a school to perform well in the first place—and then get disappointed by its ultimate performance. These schools are never expected to excel, never expected to meet basic minimum standards that are set by the various states, although sometimes they do. And when they do, *that* is a shock, not the other way around.[9]

The real kicker here is that other factors—some mentioned earlier—indicate whether a school is cool or not. These schools fail by that criterion, too. What do teachers have to do with it? One could argue teachers aren't making kids do better on those indicative tests. Simple: high test scores indicate quality teaching. Teachers aren't motivating their students to reach high test scores. Low scores indicate that schools are bad. Teachers, therefore, are the reason our schools are bad.

Therein lies a heap of logical fallacies. Chapter 5 discusses those fallacies about testing. In detail.

8. Quality education defies cultural norms.

What this means is not exactly clear. Suffice it to say, controversy is pervasive in almost any discussion on this subject. Straight to the chase: *Some cultures emphasize the value of an education more than other cultures emphasize the value of an education.*

What?

You *know* it's true. By the year 2022 more than two-thirds of the population of the University of California will come from American Asian populations, particularly Korean and Chinese Americans, or immigrants from these countries. What's more, four years hence, those groups will constitute the largest number of students that will earn a BA degree. The projection is for advanced degrees earned by Asians to go up.[10]

Why is that?

There are two distinct possibilities: either (1) Asians are inherently smarter than other cultural groups or (2) Asians value getting an education and, therefore, work harder than other cultural groups. There is, of course, the possibility that *both* of these are true. But, for the moment, settle on one of them. Which one is it?

American Asians aren't dumb. But to conclude that their brains work better because of their cultural breeding might be a bit of a stretch. It just seems that way. Because of the more recent (say, the last fifteen years) successes of Asian Americans in higher education, lots of wisecracks centering around their IQ and brain power have been heard 'bout town. But there is absolutely no reason to assume that part of the world, because, well, it is *that* part of the world, grows smarter people.

It would also seem logical that part of the world doesn't grow harder working people, either. But cultural norms grow from traditions and throughout years and years of generational hand-me-downs. *My father earned a doctorate; his father got his masters; and his father was the first in the family to go to college and get his BA degree. Education matters in our family. It matters to me. It will matter to my children. And their children, too.*

It is more likely that cultural values have a greater impact on the successes of Asians than do their naked brains. Not to dismiss the power of being inherently intelligent, but native intelligence can be wasted—and often *is* wasted—by those who are too lazy to do anything constructive with that intelligence. The drive of some people to succeed generates massive amounts of adrenaline in the classroom. They use that adrenaline to move forward, to break through the common inertia that impedes the success of others, those who are less motivated to succeed.[11]

Hispanic Americans and black Americans do not possess an equal amount of motivation to receive an education—not equal to Asians. Not many sociologists or politicians eagerly voice the truth of the matter. They don't—won't. This issue has become the naked emperor. Everybody knows he's not wearing anything; everybody stares at his nakedness every day, but nobody wants to point it out.

Cultural holdback: You act white if you speak grammatically correct English. Lots of people who aren't white sound educated. They speak in the proper syntax. They write sentences that quickly get to the point. But if they don't speak broken English, brogue, or Ebonics or misspell every other word, they are acting white. *Acting white* is pejorative. You shouldn't act white. You betray your culture, your race, your people. Translation: look and sound dumb, and you will know who you are. More important, you will fit in.

Slavery and the Alamo: They are both alive and well today, thank you. Many blacks—and guilt-ridden white people—are still writhing from the lingering effects of slavery from 150 years ago. The bondage of yesteryear lingers in the minds of the many who can't, for whatever prudent reason, let go; thus, they are (allow themselves to be) held back in all walks of life: everything, from being the first to go to college in their family, to nailing that minimum wage job at the neighborhood fast-food joint.

For a minority of Hispanics, particularly *some* Mexican Americans, the outcry to take back the land that was legitimately theirs still permeates their thinking. Thank God for the Alamo, which provides a sense of dignity in defeat; Davy Crockett was a brave, fight-to-the-death frontier hero, not a dirty rotten murdering capitalist racist piece of dung. Oh, yeah. And a coward: that Davy Crockett was a coward!

Kids are growing up with the wrong version of the story. Or maybe it is the right reason. Maybe the right version isn't known. Nobody has a monopoly on the truth of the Alamo—of what happened two hundred years ago on a dry piece of land in Texas. But *which version of the securing and development of land in the western United States is better to believe for the health and unity of our country?* That question should not be difficult to answer.

Economic diversion: Like other segments of the population, Hispanic families believe in the importance of hard work. Sometimes it is hard work—*only hard work*—that stands between feeding their families and starvation. Most Hispanic American men and women will take on any job in order to feed and shelter their families. Sometimes those families are extended big-time but, culturally speaking, a responsibility exists to feed and shelter those family members, too.

A certain nobility of this philosophy shouts for recognition; the hard reality is that children who are put to work in menial, under-the-table jobs can't be in two or three places at the same time. Their parents dissuade them from attending school under the guise of meeting their family responsibilities. Sometimes these responsibilities are babysitting small children in the family while the mother and father are working or doing housework that has been neglected for weeks because of other commitments.

If you ask Hispanics if they think educating their kids is important, almost to a person they will tell you that they believe in the value of schooling and planning for their kids' future. Like others before them, they want better for their children than they have for themselves. But they will say their families come first; they are not looking for luxuries or extras. They are seeking subsistence.[12]

Climate of failure: Americans who have been here forever find it difficult to understand the climate of failure that surrounds men, women, and children in minority communities. They point to great strides that have taken place during the last fifty years in this country.[13] Much of what kids hear from their elders is negative: *Why bother to work hard? Why study so much? Why go to college?* In the end, these parents believe their children will fail.

Some will call it institutional racism; others will label the obstacle economic deprivation. Few will call it what it probably is, a culture of failure, one that spawns a mood of failure, a fear of failing, and a self-fulfilling prophesy that ultimately leads to a sociological disaster.

"It's a white man's world," many of these parents lament to their kids. You have to work harder than anybody else to succeed. You have to be better than the white man." Or worse: "It's a white man's world. You can't win for losing. No matter what you do, how hard you work, how lucky you may get, the white man will hold you down."

Under any one of those provisions, a child faces more than just an uphill climb in school; he must contend with the negativism of family at a time when most children in America have at least *some* family support. Minority children have a vision of success that sits at the end of a long, winding path; they encounter obstacles and challenges.

If they take advantage of the opportunities afforded all Americans, they will have an equal chance of achieving their goals. Others have proven this: blacks, Latinos, Asians—others have shown it can happen.

But try *not* having that optimistic vision, that frame of mind: it's difficult for an adult; for a child, it is lethal.

Zero-sum support: Dave's thirteen-year-old son was told by his teacher that he had failed a big history test. Dave knew better. He had studied tediously, reviewed relentlessly, for the big exam. When he received his core, a 49, he knew something was wrong. Had the score been reported as a 79, he would have sloughed it off, figured he hadn't concentrated very well, or simply messed up on the test. But a 49? Nope. This had to be investigated.

But Dave's son's teacher refused to entertain the notion she had made a mistake in grading his test and told him that he should concentrate on another test, one that was coming up in a couple of weeks.

When his boy told Dave about this, Dave went straight to the teacher for clarification. He and his son's teacher discovered that she had incorrectly entered scores into her computer's grading program. With an immediate minor adjustment, Dave and the history teacher rectified the problem.

This was terrific for Dave's son. But not every boy and girl in a public school has a "Dave" for their dad; in fact, a significant number of kids have no dads at all, let alone one as supportive and protective as Dave.

Especially in inner city and rural schools, children have to fend for themselves. They often lose their will, their desire, because hardly anyone else seems to care about them—or how well they are performing in their classes. Teachers and counselors can intervene; ultimately, though, it comes down to the amount of support children have at home.

Parents must remind children daily of their duties and responsibilities. They must provide consequences if their children are not doing their part to help themselves. They must remind their kids that life is a grind; getting their education is part of that grind.

No one is home to feed this kind of wisdom to these children. Their support from family and friends adds up to a big zero; in fact, there may be negative pushback when it comes to schooling. Friends and family members who didn't attend school themselves—or tried school but later dropped out—may be contending with their own jealousies and insecurities. Another friend or family member who is succeeding in something—school, for instance—is the last thing they want to hear about. It makes them look bad. So they nag and cajole the more industrious and harder working among their family into not going to classes, not doing their homework—maybe not going to school at all.

They may encourage their family members to drop out of school, so they can get a job and support the family . . . or take care of the little ones while their parents are out doing God knows what.[14]

Disdain for authority: Cops, politicians, parents, preachers, and teachers are authority figures. They come as part of an establishment that these children have been told for years doesn't care about them, doesn't have their best interests at heart. Now these children are being told—usually by others outside their family or circle of friends—to trust authority; that these people, those they have grown to loathe, really do have their best interests at heart and will lead them to success.

An entire generation of children, most of them in minority neighborhood schools, hate teachers. They disdain teachers because, like cops and parents and politicians and preachers, teachers set strict boundaries; they make outrageous demands.

Children rebel. What they don't quite understand, of course, is that their rebellion hurts *them* far worse than it hurts those who are trying to help them. They don't get the connection between strict rules and success, or seemingly outrageous rules and success. They haven't drawn a link between trusting those they have been taught to distrust and why following rules right now is best for their future.

And schools suffer. Schools of predominantly black and Hispanic children, at all grade levels, in all corners of the United States, lose out to ignorance. They crumble at the feet of serious sociological problems that can't be solved by impulsive sweeping legislation or building a wall that Mexico allegedly will pay for.

While waiting for Superman to fly into these schools and save the day, the public might want to remember that thousands of regular teachers sweat and bleed and cry every day of every week of every year. They do so with a sense of being scorned and misunderstood, knowing they may never be fairly treated, or compensated, for what they contribute to society.

Minority students have good reason to dis their education and loathe their schools. These schools, populated by children from African American and Hispanic backgrounds, are shams. The education community should be ashamed of these decaying fortresses of perdition and ashamed of those who have allowed them to exist.

Not for a moment should *anyone* conclude that it is America's teachers who are to blame for these conditions. In a teacher's day, chock-full of orders, ordinations, and ordeals, there is little time for political posturing. A teacher's job is not to posture but to impart their knowledge and wisdom.

Teachers can't pound nails, erect walls, or tear down socioeconomic barriers that have existed since long before they were born. But they can do what they do well, what they do best—teach kids.

There are no safe zones in these war zones: The trendiness of college aside—as dumb as it may be, that trendiness—the clamor for "safe zones" on college campuses is a sad joke. Asking for places where young people are free from feeling offended is an inane misplacement of priorities. The absence of *real* safe zones on many elementary, middle school, and high school campuses in the inner city, makes those brats at Princeton look like overly educated, out-of-touch, nincompoops.

A safe zone, to most people, has little to do with scrawling *Donald Trump* in chalk on an obscure wall on a college campus; *here* a safe zone has everything to do with finding a place where you might avoid blazing bullets and flying fists on a short stroll from your classroom to the cafeteria.

Violence, thievery, and destruction of property happen at these schools on a regular basis. In Los Angeles, consistent occurrences of warfare between (and within) rival gangs of Hispanic teenagers and black teenagers are the norm, not the rarities.

After a huge brawl broke out on a campus in South L.A., dozens of the student combatants were suspended. But the surprise came when school officials discovered that much of the disturbance was not caused by students at the school, but by outsiders who walked onto campus with the sole intent of agitating. Another fight, at Sylmar High School, turned out to be part of a race war.[15]

This kind of thing—outside agitators who instigate racial divide and gang warfare—astounded even the most astute observers. But it shouldn't have. There is enough anger in these communities to go around. There is enough deprivation to impact these kids for a long, long time. There is enough envy to spur acts of violence. The school was ripe for upheaval. The blame, if there were any to be placed, should have been leveled at school-district officials for allowing conditions on campus that humiliated the children into acting like caricatures of cultural stereotypes.

The two groups of students, those on the lowest rungs of the socioeconomic ladder, fought each other. They achieved nothing, of course, but a whole heck of a lot of bad media publicity—and their eventual dismissals from school.

Beyond that—unfortunately, there is a *beyond*—the crime statistics at these places are staggering: rape—up, theft—up, property damage—up, assault—up, and *murder*—up. Who would want to attend school at these bastions of brutality if they didn't *have* to attend?

Don't blame it on America's teachers. They are pawns. Politicians and education administrators move them around at will and sacrifice whatever they feel compelled to sacrifice; those politicians and education administrators make a play, just to impress upon others that they are doing *their* jobs. They want the public to take the bait, to bite at the first offering they see and assume there is a lot more where that came from. But there isn't.

A child who plays in a yard where he sniffs the acrid stench of gunpowder in the air doesn't get a chance at living his life to the fullest—or living a full life. A child who comes from a home in which a drunken boyfriend regularly beats the snot out of his mother doesn't suit himself up in the morning, rush enthusiastically out of the house, and burst into a classroom, eager to dissect the poetry of Robert Frost. It doesn't work that way. It can't. It's not the teachers' fault. A sociological cancer such as this has nothing to do with teachers.

1. A twofold repair of inner city schools must come from America's leaders.

Because an entire book could be—and should be—written on the subject of lousy schools, the ensuing brevity may not do the topics justice. However, it could plant a seed of enlightenment. And that would be a good start.

2. Federal money should pour into those raunchy areas.

Raunchy areas?

These kids need money to be spent on them—more than other kids do. It doesn't matter where the money comes from (how it is raised), which programs are cut, or how the dough is distributed. *It simply has to be.* People can raise objections, scream holy hell, all day and all night long—to no end. The money must come. Yes, the federal government already distributes nifty grants to special-education programs and to school-lunch programs for disadvantaged kids. That's terrific.

Now it has to do more.

Besides having equipment and books and computer technology, our lousy schools may attract more teachers, maybe even better ones. Teachers who initially volunteer to work at these ramshackle sites will be favorably compensated for their extraordinary efforts, for their bravery. It isn't exactly clear where Superman is, but if he really exists, he will probably follow the money.

It doesn't take a rocket scientist to understand that money alone won't do jack for these schools. Serious obstacles to these unfortunate children's receiving an adequate education cling to the system, and not many of them have to do with money. But money is a start. It buys stuff. Money buys materials kids need in order to learn and teachers need in order to teach.

While throwing the word *money* around . . .

3. Parents should have a choice as to where their kids go to school.

Yeah, yeah. The teachers unions hate school-choice vouchers.[16] They despise the idea of making their people compete in order to attract students. They fear that some schools will simply dry up and die if school choice is ever established on a mass scale.

Hey, Bobby, you want to go to that school where those kids got molested by their teachers?

Not really, Mama. Do I have a choice?

Yes.

Then—no.

Teachers unions think their collective bargaining chips might fall off the table in a school-vouchers program. The unions abhor teachers being judged for competency against other teachers. The most competent teachers aren't union officials. They don't want to be judged

Look at this logically: if teachers wish not to be vilified for what is happening to destroy America's schools, they need to do their part, make more sacrifices. (Sigh: *more sacrifices!*) If this means getting more qualified teachers into those classrooms, whatever is necessary must be done in order to get those teachers into those classrooms ($$$).

The tragedy: teachers can't do a lot about horrible parenting, substance abuse, crime, and hunger. Educators do what they can, when they can, while they can. Sure, most teachers would like to punch that abusive father in the nose, or rip the mustache off that neglectful mother. This makes complete sense. But it won't happen. It can't happen.

Teachers will rise to the occasion, as they usually do, to fight for, and defend, the young people they have committed their lives to making better. They won't get much attention. The praises won't be coming their way. But almost every teacher in America knew what he was getting into when he signed up to become a teacher.

And he was crazy enough to go through with it, anyway.

NOTES

1. Caucasian and Asian students are typically not counted as minorities, even when they are broken down into subcategories: Italian, German, Japanese, Korean, and so on. According to politically correct dogma, white students have never been persecuted, and Asian students . . . well, Asian students are rich and smart—*really* rich, and *really* smart (which, of course, they all are not, but so goes the stereotype).

2. *National Study for Education Statistics*, 2016, May 2015, http://nces.ed.gov/programs/coe/indicator_cge.asp .

3. Alan Singer, "Why Many Inner City Schools Function Like Prisons," Huffpost Education, December 15, 2014, http://www.huffingtonpost.com/alan-singer/why-many-inner-city-schoo_b_5993626.html .

4. Bruce Gevirtzman, *An Intimate Understanding of America's Teenagers* (Westport, CT: Praeger, 2008), 207–8.

5. Edjoin.org. Research performed on this website on May 31, 2016, indicated that the majority of vacancies, particularly in math and science in the secondary schools, and in grades one to three in elementary schools, were in urban areas of the country. This varies from year to year, but your author's suspicions were right. Thank you—though it did not exactly take a rocket scientist to figure this out.

6. Mr. Ratzfield's dilemma is shared by teachers across the country. To a lesser degree, it's like that of a teacher who has almost two hundred students throughout her day and silently prays that most of them do not turn in their essays, which she must read, grade, and return. Damned if they do, and damned if they don't—though mostly damned when they do.

7. Sarah D. Sparks and Caralee J. Adams, "High School Poverty Levels Tied to College-Going," *Education* Week, October 22, 2013, http://www.edweek.org/ew/articles/2013/10/23/09college.h33.html: summary of article.

8. A class from an upscale, economically advantaged neighborhood should take a field trip to one of *these* schools. They should do it around the Thanksgiving holiday. One look, a short feel for a school in the slums . . . the ungrateful, obnoxious complaining would stop. Thanksgiving would have a specific focus.

9. Jessica Campbell, "Why Poor Black Children Succeed at This Brooklyn Middle School," *Dominion*, January 3, 2013, Social Justice Section. The school boasts of an especially demanding curriculum and extremely strict regulations. Educators say it works here, and one of the reasons is that the school administrators wouldn't take "I can't" for an answer.

10. "More than Half of Asians in U.S. Have a Bachelor's Degree or Higher," *United States Census Newsroom*, March 29, 2016, CB-16-56.

11. Nicholas Kristof, "The Asian Advantage," *New York Times*, Sunday Review, October 10, 2015. This op-ed columnist cites two major reasons for Asians' success in American schools: the maintenance of two-parent households and historical cultural reverence for education institutions.

12. Jens Manuel Krogstad, "5 Facts about Latinos and Education," *Factank*, May 26, 2015, http://www.pewresearch.org/fact-tank/2015/05/26/5-facts-about-latinos-and-education/.

13. Not another country in the world in all of history has ever passed sweeping legislation that made it illegal to be racist. The 1964 Civil Rights Law had an immediate impact on American institutions, such as the schools; and it had a long-term impact on American individuals, like Uncle Billy.

14. Only God may know what, but here's a guess: drugs and alcohol are rampant in these neighborhoods. Crack cocaine used to be the drug of choice, but now it's heroine and cheaper concoctions of cocaine. Any kind of booze will do—the cheaper, the better, but also the more dangerous. When fathers—and oftentimes mothers—come home from a binge, they ain't ready to vie for a "Parent of the Year" award.

15. "Black vs. Mexican: Sylmar High School Students Race War On," *Los Angeles Times*, May 13, 2016, News, 1.

16. Joy Pullman, "Teachers' Union Threatens to Sue Private Schools Over Voucher Program," *Daily Caller*, August 2, 2012, School reform News, http://dailycaller.com/2012/08/02/louisiana-teachers-union-threatens-to-sue-private-schools-over-voucher-program/.

Chapter Twelve

Forbidden Territory

If you are about to have dinner or getting ready to go to bed for the night, skip this part; in fact, if you have been having nightmares, you ought to consider passing by this chapter of the book.

The American media have not been kind to teachers. Tarnishing teachers' images isn't something that would make any American particularly proud of himself. That isn't a goal, something a person sets out to do in the morning.

Parents have no ill will toward their own kids' teachers; in fact, in most cases, the opposite is true: they want to think their kids' teachers are the best thing since sliced bread (even though sliced bread isn't such a novelty anymore; how about the best thing since the invention of the iPod)?

Unless there is an incident involving their child, or until the child or parent perceives a gross injustice occurred in the classroom that impacted the child in a negative way, most parents assume the teacher is passable. The parent may not be running to the mountaintops and yelling the teacher's name with wilder enthusiasm than the Cramer family displayed during a round of *Family Feud*, but that parent would respond to questions about his kid's teacher in a manner that showed the teacher in a favorable light.[1]

The climate that prompted the research and compilation of a strong defense for America's teachers was *so ugly, so distasteful, so unfair, so unrepresentative, and so misleading*, that there was no other choice but to defend teachers. Not to do overkill on what has already been articulated: America's teachers have achieved unprecedented, unheard-of successes in a multicultural, multiracial, multi-everything-you-can-imagine-and-more environment, often working under unfavorable conditions, cowering to the sometimes ridiculous, unreasonable whims of administrative supervisors who wouldn't know what a good classroom looked like if their lives depended on it.

Imagine going through life with the mission of bringing down the men and women who teach our children. They're out there, those people. Yes, they are.[2] But they aren't the primary problem; those who inadvertently diminish teachers continue to do most of the damage—but forgive them, for they know not what they do!

Some teachers have done awful things. The law requires an investigation of anyone planning to work with children. The FBI investigates prospective Little League coaches.[3] All states require fingerprints upon the employment of new teachers. These laws have been in effect for years. When a felony, a misdemeanor, or an arrest pops up on the radar screen, the antennae on district administrators go up. Committing felonies disqualifies people from working in the teaching profession.

Because arrest records may be expunged, administrators do not have direct access to those records. In a nation where an arrested individual is innocent until declared guilty by a judge or jury, arrest records shouldn't mean a lot, not officially. But where kids are involved, there is hypersensitivity around arrest records. When a man is *suspected* of harming a child in a violent or sexual way, the criminal justice system springs into action. The presumption of innocence, a concept of paramount importance in the criminal justice system, no longer has a place. Men and women who are suspected of hurting kids—much less *arrested* for it—suddenly find themselves in a unique position of jurisprudence.

In the United States of America, *in a court of law, a man who sits awaiting trial is presumed innocent of the crime he has been accused of until proven guilty of that crime.*

A man, presumed to be innocent *until proven guilty* of that crime, sits in a courtroom: the wording is subtle. Separate from its context, it is easy to see how someone might be led along the path of assuming, eventually, that the original presumption (that of innocence) will be inextricably linked to a preordained verdict (that of guilt). It's all a matter of time, a formality of procedure.

Throughout the years, however, American courts have managed successfully to step around this misdirected subtlety and live up to the intent of the presumption of innocence, a hallmark quality of American democracy. The media try time and time again to convict men who have been arrested for despicable crimes; yet, in hushed tones, someone whispers, "He's innocent until proven guilty." As though this proclamation diminishes the assumption that this guy obviously committed the dastardly deed.

And there is no patience or empathy for these people, either. Brian Palmer wrote, "Convicts who have committed crimes against children, especially sexual abuse, are hated, harassed, and abused. Many inmates refer to molesters as 'dirty' prisoners, and some insist that assaulting or killing them represents a service to society."[4]

In 1983, a small quiet, unassuming preschool in the southern tip of Los Angeles County became the focal point for one of the most sensationalized trials in American history: the McMartin Preschool case, embroidered with cries of rape, molestation, witches, animal sacrifice, and other perversions so sinister that they were not detailed on a daily basis in the reporting of the *Los Angeles Times*.[5]

The famous case, the most expensive trial ever, dragged on for seven years and ended without any convictions. Two of the defendants, the main ones, were retried. One was acquitted, the other's case ended in a mistrial. The end result brought no one to justice because the allegations were so ludicrous and the events described so preposterous.

But that didn't stop analysts. They had a field day with the McMartin case. If nothing else, criminologists and journalists delved into the whys of the case, wondering about the absurd nature of the charges and how they had ever gotten so far, the case being almost a decade long.

Excluding most of the particulars, it is important to examine the main reasons why this case ended in an acquittal, with eight of the defendants exonerated, save one, who was not convicted. These principles are crucial to understanding one of the most unfair, disgusting debasements of the teaching profession:

1. *The case broke with the allegations of a nutty woman.*

Martha Scott[6] thought something was happening at the school. She reported it to the police. She later recanted, but that didn't matter to the national media. She was portrayed as a kook. She was a kook. The longer the trial went—it went for a *long* time—the nuttier that woman sounded.

2. *Hysteria took over.*

Hysteria is how the case mushroomed. Children were being molested. Children were being hurt. There was one, no—two, no—*eight* teachers involved. They were playing awful, vulgar games in closets, hiding from parents when they came to pick up their kids. Eventually, there came talk of animal sacrifices and children riding naked on horseback down Mulholland Boulevard.

3. *Political motives became obvious.*

Once the prosecution was in, it was *in*. There had to be a certain point during the course of the proceedings (after two years, maybe) where one of the prosecutors (Lael Rubin,[7] maybe) went to District Attorney Robert Philibosian and said, "You know, Bob, this is stupid. These allegations are absurd. We won't be able to prove *any* of them. And even if we could, no one would believe us. In the end, we are going to look like bumbling fools."[8]

There *had* to have been that moment, that meeting.

There wasn't.

The prosecutors weighed the pros and cons of continuing the case. Perhaps the embarrassment of losing a long, bitter court battle was more face saving than dropping the case outright.

They may have spared their dignity by not going forward with a second trial, but, nope, *what the hell . . . we're already in!* Lives were ruined, the school closed forever, and the credibility of the Los Angeles District Attorney's Office had taken a big licking.

4. *The allegations were far-fetched.*

Cats cut open: that was a big one. Blood and guts of brutal animal sacrifice while the kids watched: that piqued some interest. Animal bones, including those of a dead horse, buried on the school site, though they were never found, even after extensive excavation, brought the media to a frenzy; and KABC News anchor Wayne Sachs, crawling fresh out of the woodwork, managed to disseminate inside information (that he got from one of the prosecution's star witnesses).[9]

But nothing ever came of those late, weird embellishments. Nothing. It made for some pretty hairy sensationalism. But that was about all it made for, the whole thing crossing the border of probable into laughable a long time before the case was over.

5. *Videotapes hurt the prosecution.*

Actual video testimony from children at the preschool describing the hideous things that were done to them by their teachers could have provided a smoking gun for the prosecution. The problem: on those tapes, jurors watched, and heard, the children being *coerced* into answering questions in a manner to satisfy the prosecution's case. The children were led to specific responses and then coached to repeat them. Jurors eventually studied the tapes in open court sessions.

6. *Charges could not be substantiated.*

Allegations were never specifically corroborated. Drinking blood, killing animals, and leaving the school for burial ceremonies, far-fetched and inane, never lent themselves to finding witnesses to corroborate any of that.

7. *The defendants elicited sympathy.*

Only Raymond Buckey, admittedly a tad weird and creepy looking, fit the profile of a "typical child molester." The others, mostly matronly old ladies who worked feverishly hard to keep the school running smoothly, defied the stereotypes. Looking at Buckey's grandmother, the founder of the McMartin School, was an exercise in exasperation. Wondering how this woman was about to lose her life savings, her school, and her reputation made for fascinating print and video media, but it did not make for a sense of fairness and justice in the world.

8. Sensationalism eventually hurt the state's case.

People got sick of this case. It went on for years.[10] TV news covered it ad nauseam. People wanted the trial to be over so badly that they were willing to rush a verdict, though years of trial could hardly be fittingly labeled, "rushing a verdict." They wanted a faster verdict—and preferred an acquittal.

9. The chief defendant's appearance changed.

At the beginning of the trial, Raymond Buckey resembled a sleazy, lecherous, unmarried child molester. By the end of the trial, he resembled a lawyer, dressed in smart suits and classy ties, a pair of intellectual-appearance-enhancing glasses. He carried his body upright, promoting an air of confidence. He had a girlfriend who sat behind him throughout most of his ordeal. Who was going to convict a guy who looked like that for the crimes he was accused?

10. Guilty teachers became the unpopular view.

Most cases of abuse in our nation's schools are not nearly as sensationalistic as those reported at the McMartin school. People currently perceive that school abuse cases are rapidly increasing. The Internet has brought notoriety to cases that never before would have been discovered, let alone talked about. One could cynically argue that these types of abuses *have* occurred in the past, but nobody found out about them. Or they did find out, but kept quiet. The most cynical explanation of all is that abuse cases weren't reported by local school sites or by parents. Or . . . those cases never got beyond the local school board and (gulp) the teachers unions.

From 2014 to 2016 in the Los Angeles Unified School District, there were at least three blockbuster molestation cases that involved alleged fondling, caressing, and the drinking of semen. Parents of the victims in one of those cases won an eighty-million-dollar judgment against the school district. The money to pay off the suits comes out of the pockets of L.A. taxpayers.

Robert Manly, an attorney for the parents of these alleged abuse victims, said in an interview, "All teachers are taking the blame for this . . . and we know that's not fair. It was a small handful of teachers. . . . But what about the administrators who hired these people and [possibly] knew what was going on [and covered it up]? To whom will *they* become accountable?" (italics added).[11]

Mark Berndt[12] sits in prison. Meanwhile, the teachers union, which argued that he was still legally entitled to his retirement money, even if convicted, and administrators at the schools involved (three defendants in three different schools) walk free today, many of them still collecting their six-figure salaries.

This perverted man was *assigned by officials* to a position where he gained the trust and admiration of very young children—and then breached that trust in the most egregious of ways.

The bewilderment of the parents of children who were victimized by Berndt can't be emphasized enough: the largest California teachers union went to bat for this alleged predator by arguing that he legally be able to collect his pension.

Get this: not only would an alleged predator (keep in mind he initially admitted to the allegations) gather his retirement (with the option of monthly installments for the rest of his life), the ACLU (who else?), in conjunction with the L.A. teachers union, is protecting his "right" to collect his health insurance benefits until the day he dies (which is what all California teachers are entitled to, says the ACLU).[13]

Every time there is something in the news about a child being harmed by a teacher, the "fit hits the sham." Which is the way it *should* be. However, the public and, unfortunately, the politicians, those who should know better, cast aspersions on *all* teachers as being child molesters or violent abusers.

That is so obviously wrong, it's painful to have to point it out.

Sexual predators should be locked up for life. It shouldn't matter whether they have a history of abuse or have committed other crimes; it doesn't matter if they are the best teachers in the history of civilization. What matters is the crime and the veracity of the accusation. What matters is whether the suspect merits an investigation, an arrest, and, ultimately, a trial.

With sexual abuse and teachers, the presumption of innocence flies out the window. The teacher is forced to prove a negative. (*I* didn't *touch her when she stopped by after class to ask me a question.*) And proving a negative is next to impossible. That's why presumption of innocence exists for other types of cases. Innocent people would wind up in prison—or worse—because of the difficulty of proving a negative.

Molestation/abuse situations may be exaggerated by the media; they may—as in the McMartin case—be fueled by hysteria with little or no legitimate foundation behind them. But public sentiment in these cases is to err on the side of safety: the benefit of the doubt goes to the child. If a teacher molests a kid, throw him in prison and drop the keys to his cell down the toilet. (Your humble author is not averse to executing child molesters of a certain ilk, but that would be a subject for a different book.) That said, here are several clarifications for those concerned to sort out this sensitive, sociological dilemma:

1. The number of reported abuse cases is surprisingly miniscule.

A review of statistics that are kept on abuse and molestation in the schools may illuminate the situation. But some facts are difficult to analyze: kids abusing other kids appears in those statistics. Adult-to-child crime data become distorted when statistics include high school boys staking out the girls at the local junior high school are figured into the equation.

Taking into consideration the number of teachers in the United States, over 3.1 million,[14] and the reported abuse incidents over a five-year period, the percentage of teachers accused of molestation or violence against children is less than one-fiftieth of 1 percent. The conviction rates are lower than that: .00012 percent[15]

Even *one* actual molester is bad enough. But given the large numbers in the profession, and the undeniable access to kids teachers possess, your eight-year-old son has a greater chance of being killed by a car slamming into him while you are dropping him off at school than he does of being molested by his schoolteacher.[16]

2. Teachers are not afraid to condemn their own.

Any teacher would sooner knock the head off another teacher before she would allow him to hurt a child. Typical outrage expressed by teachers is normally quieted by administrators; but when asked by media outlets to comment on the subject of abuse, teachers did not hesitate. The teachers who expressed themselves here are fed up with the broad-brush approach the media take toward the teaching profession. The issue of molestation is particularly galling because of its despicable implications.

> If I suspect something is going on with the kids, something isn't right, I talk about it with my supervisors. . . . I don't take chances. . . . I would err on the side of safety. Kids, all the kids, don't have anyone to protect them but us. We can hurt them, or we can save them. If we don't save them, then what's left?
> —Sandra, fourth-grade special education

> Some teachers, you know, they look at things through rose-colored glasses, or they stick their heads in the sand. . . . He was a substitute teacher, young, attractive, and the girls liked him. They liked him too much, and he knew it. He took advantage of it. What started out as running, jogging, excursions, soon turned into more than that. . . . The strange thing was . . . there were four girls involved, and none of the girls said anything, until one of them got pregnant. They were protecting him. That's what was so strange.
> —Cloris, eighth-grade

To a man—or a woman—teachers place blame where blame is due. Professions that don't, that protect their own for the purpose of brotherhood, lose credibility with the public. They also lose credibility with their fellow lawyers. There's quite a pair of matched words: *lawyer, credibility*.

3. *Newspaper sales trump truth.*

All forms of media, including the Internet, report *the* events that catch the fancy of the American public—sometimes people can't get enough. Celebrity stories serve that purpose. So do accounts of terrorist attacks. In the last election cycle, presidential debates brought media attention; record numbers of Americans watched cable news for the first time. All of these *sell*. But so do stories that describe sinister events involving children. Children up the ante. Wherever there may be peril, where children exist, the peril gets magnified.

> *Female Teacher Seduces Male Student at After-Prom Party.*
> A female art teacher who often spent extra hours working with her students . . .
>
> *Allegations of Fondling Turn to Full-Blown Charges of Sexual Assault*
> An eighth-grade student at Farmer Junior High had repeatedly told school officials . . .
>
> *Parents Allege Sex Games During Recess*
> Several parents at Holden Elementary School have reported unusual activity . . .

Headlines like these sell products. They foster discussions in bars and encourage tweets and Internet posts. Everybody has an opinion about teachers who molest children. The age-old blind trust from parents, when betrayed, is the thing that popular stories are made of.

What gets lost is the concept of presumption of innocence. Media sources do not directly state that a teacher is guilty of sexual assault. They do not consciously detract from the presumption of innocence. But they wind up denying this presumption, anyway. The boldface cries by media about illicit sexual misconduct, their almost gleeful reporting of disgusting, sensational crimes by America's teachers, is the next best thing to reporting the misconduct of Catholic priests.

4. *Monitoring teacher misconduct is currently a high priority.*

Even with all the attention on teachers, most educators maintain a strong defensive posture that usually protects them from wrongful accusations. In recent years, small things have meant a lot. A surprising number of those small things are within the control of the teacher:

- Do not be alone with a student in a classroom
- Keep classroom doors wide open when alone with a student
- Never give a student a ride in your car
- Choose language wisely when complimenting a student
- Understand that a student's pain and frustration invoke irrational behaviors
- Do not engage in physical combat with a student
- Stay off students' social media pages; bar students from yours
- Keep both incoming and sent e-mail messages, especially from students and parents
- Avoid profanity around students
- Refrain from complimenting your students' appearance
- Avoid hugging and touching students
- Use discretion when showing students films with sexual content
- Do not single a student out as being sexy or especially attractive
- In front of students, refrain from talking about your personal dating habits
- In front of students, refrain from talking about your sexual exploits

And then there is common sense. Not everything can be covered here. Things come up that could not have been anticipated. Teachers need to keep an eye on issues that are brought up in the media and concerns voiced by the public. That's where it is now. Hugging is forbidden. Sad. But that's what it's come to.

The public can be assured that teachers are on guard. They will bite their own if they have to in order to protect a kid. They put children as their highest priority. It should be clear that teachers are willing to defy their unions if they think children are not being protected. Let it be clear that teachers will not put up with their unions going to bat for child molesters. They don't care what their unions' obligations are. Kids come first. Teaching is about children. Teachers know that Nelson Mandela spoke the truth and that it takes a very special person to fully understand his point: "There can be no keener revelation of a society's soul than the way in which it treats its children."[17]

5. Alleged obscene teacher behavior has become a scapegoat.

Your children hate school. They are failing their classes: Your second grader has been unable to master math concepts, is falling behind, way behind what others say should be the norm. Your high school senior won't graduate. His government teacher has sent you notices about his impending failure. Homework, the teacher says, has been your kid's Achilles heel. He never does his homework.

You don't want to believe your children are awful students. You think they are equal to others when it comes to ability. You are a supportive parent. You provide help to your children. You sit down with them and help them with their homework. You hire tutors. You contact their teachers. You respond to teachers' e-mails and phone calls. So, what's wrong here?

It must be the teacher's fault. The teachers haven't done their part. America's teachers aren't what they used to be. They don't know what to teach anymore—or how to teach it—there have been so many changes in curriculum, trends, and teaching styles. Maybe your kids' teachers have become victims, too.

You complain about teachers to anyone who will listen. They are failing the public. They are failing the children. Because of the deterioration of the teaching profession, America is in trouble. The future looks dim. Your children's future is in jeopardy.

Does anyone know about this? Does anyone care? The rest of society seems so blasé about the problems facing kids in the schools. They don't understand what teachers have been through. But it doesn't matter—not a bit.

Someone has to take the fall.

Those teachers are not only uneducated; they are incompetent. But it's worse, much worse. They are immoral. Whenever they get the chance, they do the unthinkable. They take advantage of children. Perversion supersedes self-control. Where there is perversion, there is little self-control. That is why so many young men attain teaching positions. They gain access. Once they have gained access, their perversions manifest themselves. Why else would a man want to hang around several dozen little children all day? For what reason would a grown man stick himself into a confined space with thirty-five drooling, sniffling seven-year-olds?

Access.

The once-respected, esteemed position of schoolteacher is a ready scapegoat for most that is wrong in our nation's schools.

Three interesting—maybe fascinating—cases of alleged abuse highlight the ambiguity of recent allegations.

In Alabama, thirty-eight-year-old Matthew Shane Webster, a former Cleveland High School math teacher, was indicted in January 2015 on one count of a school employee having sexual contact with a student under the age of nineteen. Five months later, Webster married the woman involved, Amy Cox.

After their marriage, Mrs. Webster said she would refuse to testify against Mr. Webster, citing spousal privilege protection. The court, however, proclaimed that Mrs. Webster wasn't protected by spousal privilege, suggesting such a privilege doesn't exist in cases where one spouse is the victim of the other.

Cox was eighteen, a legal adult in Alabama. Their relationship was consensual, if, in fact, it existed at all. Amy Cox and Matthew Webster simply could deny the sexual nature of their relationship. Perhaps, there wasn't one.

They got married. If a statute had been broken, the teacher should have been fired. But arrested? Made into some sort of satanic figure?[18] Portrayed as a demon? They were, after all, adults.

This case made the news. Nobody died. This teacher used poor judgment, no doubt. He should have been removed from the classroom, at least until the conclusion of an investigation. The weight of the crime should determine the consequences, not hysteria or vindictiveness.

In Palo Alto, California, a teacher was suspended for allegedly having a relationship with a former student—and then marrying her. Her parents complained that she had a sexual affair with her English teacher, in his forties, *while she was his student*. However, both the teacher and the student denied that this occurred. They were involved together in several school-related activities but did not, according to *both* of them, engage in a physical or romantic relationship.

Because they admitted they had begun dating after she graduated, and were later married, the case picked up some steam. She was eighteen during the time they were alleged to have engaged in the relationship. But the case took an interesting twist along the way.

The Graff report, an investigation into the matter by the school district, stated, "A credible strong suspicion that a sexual relationship may have occurred soon after graduation, and a credible strong suspicion there may have been behavior or interactions that desensitized the student while she was a student to the potential of a future sexual relationship, raise serious concerns that justify continued proactive and preventative work by the District in this area."[19]

What the *heck* does "desensitized the student," mean, anyway? Really. This kind of mumbo jumbo hangs a teacher's life in the balance. The report goes on to say, "[She] denied that a romantic relationship ever formed. Accordingly, we do not have sufficient direct evidence to conclude that a sexual relationship transpired."[20]

Which is significant, especially when it comes to the law. There is no legality associated with "desensitized." The conclusion: "We are left with a credible strong suspicion that behavior between [them] was more friendly than either admitted during interviews, but the preponderance of the evidence does not support a conclusion that any behavior rose to a level of sexual harassment of [the female student] or unwelcome behavior during the time she was a student."

The teacher was immature. He was probably setting something up for the future, after she graduated from high school. But she was eighteen, of legal age, and after graduation she was free to pursue her relationships, even with a former teacher. One may question the morality of a forty-something teacher "grooming" an eighteen-year-old student for a future relationship, but . . . *they did get married.* And before they married, they did not engage in sexual relations (again, according to both of them).[21]

Let's untangle this mess about sexual abuse of students by teachers:

1. Abuse (molestation) is rare—practically imperceptible.
2. Teachers, as a whole, disdain it.
3. The predators are jailed, their careers over.
4. There is a place in hell (not just teacher hell, such as Friday faculty meetings) for a child predator.
5. Some segments of society want to think the worst about teachers.
6. The media sensationalize, well beyond the boundaries of reality.
7. Educators are taking preventative steps to stave off future incidents.
8. Molestation cases are complex and can't always be taken at face value.
9. Teachers have become scapegoats for what is wrong with education.
10. Anecdotal reporting has portrayed to the public all teachers as pedophiles.

United Teachers of Los Angeles, the union in L.A. that spent an inordinate amount of energy making sure Mark Berndt, accused of molesting numerous children at his elementary school, including the dispersement of semen-laden donuts to his students, is able to collect the aggregate of his retirement savings, argues that the union did nothing wrong. Sam Shuter said, "We did it right. We are obligated to protect a teacher's rights, and he has not been convicted of anything yet."[22]

As despicable as this sounds, Mr. Shuter is correct: no one, at that point, had been convicted of anything. And as monstrous as he may be, Mark Berndt is not the reason America lags behind other countries in math and science.

Despite the disgust that all feel about these crimes, and the loathing for these criminals—not to mention intolerance of the union's protection of hideous representatives of the teaching profession—the principles under which the nation was founded must be tempered with a legal and moral duty to protect children from the scum that would hurt them.

NOTES

1. One episode of *Family Feud* featured a family that had five teachers on the show. They lost. They were soundly thumped by a family from Georgia that looked like they could have walked out of the movie *Deliverance*. They didn't lose because they were edged out by the *Deliverance* family; they lost because they were dumber than a doornail.

2. Robert D. Ramsey, *Don't Teach the Canaries Not to Sing* (Thousand Oaks, CA: Corwin Press, 2008), 106, par. 3.

3. Hyperbole and a feeble attempt at humor—at first! But in retrospect, this is not too far from the actual truth. Youth sports coaches usually get investigated for prior criminal conduct before they are allowed to work with young people.

4. Brian Palmer, "Are Child Molesters Really the Most Hated People in Prison?" *Slate*, November 15, 2011, http://www.slate.com/articles/news_and_politics/explainer/2011/11/jerry_sandusky_out_on_bail_are_child_molesters_tormented_in_american_prisons_.html .

5. When the case hit its apex of sensationalism, the *Times* joined with other media reporting in detail as graphically as possible the allegations in this case. Back in the day, before the Internet, newspapers that reported stories detailing brutal crimes or situations involving children sold a lot of copies.

6. Not this pathetic woman's real name.

7. Lael Rubin was the lead prosecutor in the McMartin case.

8. After the second trial, District Attorney Philibosian lost his reelection bid.

9. Sachs allegedly got information from one of the leading experts in the country on child courtroom testimony. He was also allegedly boinking her. He got his story. She got him to report in a favorable light for the prosecution. They got each other. Allegedly.

10. Paul Eberle and Shirley Eberle, *The Abuse of Innocence: The McMartin Preschool Trial* (Buffalo, NY: Prometheus Books, 2003) (a summary of events). This book dragged into infinity as well, which is ironic, because it indicts the process that allowed the trial to carry on until practically everybody involved was dead, or wished they were dead.

11. KABC AM Radio, Los Angeles, "The Peter Tilden Show," April 28, 2016.

12. Not his real name.

13. *Except* for the teachers who molest little children, but that's being nitpicky.

14. National Center for Education Statistics, 2016, http://nces.ed.gov/fastfacts/display.asp?id=372 .

15. Paul G. Stuckle, "A Criminal Defense Attorney's View of False Sexual Assault," 2004, http://www.ejfi.org/Courts/Courts-22.htm. One major problem arises in attempting to arrive at an agreed-upon definition of what constitutes a sexual assault. It could be anything from rape to telling an inappropriate joke in front of a blushing student. Statistics can be tampered with and manipulated to fit agendas.

16. Hyperbole, and I have absolutely no idea how close this is to the actual statistical truth.

17. Nelson Mandela, Launch of the Nelson Mandela Children's Fund, Mahlamba Ndlopfu Pretoria South Africa, May 8, 1995.

18. Those questions should be answered. In the absence of breaking a statute or breaching a morals clause, what should happen to a pair of adults who engage in sexual behavior that deviates from the norm? And how deep should society's reprisals go? Again, these questions are not rhetorical.

19. It is critical to repeat here that *nothing of a physical nature transpired during the student/teacher relationship*. Only after she turned eighteen and had graduated was there a (alleged) physical connection. They were later married.

20. Peggy Bunker, "Palo Alto Teacher Accused of Inappropriate Relationship with Former Student Agrees to Resign for $150,000," *NBC Bay Area, Peninsula*, November 12, 2015, http://www.nbcbayarea.com/news/local/Palo-Alto-Teacher-Accused-of-Inappropriate-Relationship-Resign-347382731.html .

21. Ibid.

22. Howard Blume, "L.A. Teacher Suspected of Lewd Conduct Keeps Benefits," *Los Angeles Times*, February 1, 2012, Now, 1.

Index

ACLU, 158
Allen, Woody, 78
anti-teacher sentiment, 92–93
arrest records, 154
Asian Americans, 144–145

Baker, Grant, 117
Barber, Mr., 112–114
Bateman, Shannon, 135–136
bathroom privileges, 131–132
Berman, Richard, 87
Blackboard Jungle: description of, 1; reference to, 1, 2, 3, 4, 6
boys without fathers, 10
Brandt, Mark, 158, 164
Breaking Bad: about medical insurance, 20–21; reference to, 19, 129
Buckey, Raymond: court appearance of, 157; description of, 156
business professionals as teachers, 116–118

Calderon, Mr., 74–76
Christie, Chris, 51
class sizes, 85
climate of failure, 146–149
coal miners: compensation of, 32; creativity of, 35; death and safety hazards of, 33–34; job stagnation of, 36–37; tasks of, 30; unions of, 39
creativity, of teachers, 35–36

credentialing standards, 84–85
Cold War, 43–44
cookie cutter approach: description and analysis of, 96–98; drawbacks of, 100–101
Cox, Amy and Webster, Matthew, 162–164
Craft, Johnson, 33
Columbine massacre, 133
Common Core: drawbacks of, 102–103; definition of, 103–107; reference to, xiv, 35, 47, 63, 84, 92, 96, 102, 137
compensation, 20, 21, 23, 24, 32, 85, 126, 139
complaints by teachers, 72–74, 77

Dangerous Minds: description of, 1; reference to, 2, 4, 5, 6
degradation, 23
Dewey, John, 117
disruptive students: list of behaviors, 88–89; policies for, 89
divorce, 126
downtrodden schools: characteristics of, 139–151; drug use in, 140; poor attendance in, 140–141; sectionalization of, 139
Duster, Lily, 25

The Emperor's New Clothes, 108

167

employment of teachers: job growth, 36; job opportunities, 4; job statistics, 36–38
Escalante, Jaime. *See Stand and Deliver*
excuses, xii, xiii–xv, 107

fatigue, 18–20
financial insecurity, 126
Franklin, Benjamin, wisdom of, xii

Graff Report, on desensitization, 163
global warming, 66
great teachers: competency of, 111, 118–119; description of, 110–111; education levels of, 111; judgments by, 112–114; qualities of, 110
Grimsley, Ty, 126
gun violence in schools, 133

health and safety of teachers: compared to coal miners, 34–35; concern for, 34
Henson, Jim, xv
home schooling, 27
hopelessness, 26–27
humiliation, 23–26

inner-city schools, repair of, 150
innovations, 90–92; International Baccalaureate, 96, 101–102; No Child Left Behind, 91, 91–92, 106, 107; Second to None, 91, 106

Jacobs, Sandy, 50
Jenkins, Denise, 67
Johnson, Melbourne, 30
Jones, Mr., 122–124, 129–133

Kenson, Jack, 136

Landberry, Mike, 133
laughable premises, movies with, 6

Mandela, Nelson, 161
Manly, Robert, 157
marketable skills of coal miners, 30–32
McMartin Preschool Case: acquittal, reasons for, 155–157; description of, 155; hysteria surrounding, 155; and Martha Scott, 155; media coverage of, 156, 157; political motives, 155; reference to, 158; video tapes, of testimony, 156
Medina, Mrs.: plight of, 121, 124, 131; update on, 133
merit pay, 65, 85, 86
minority students: description of, 137, 144, 148; parental support of, 147–136
Minton, Rachael, 55
molestation: media depictions of, 90; preventative action, 161
money, impact of, 84
mortality: death rates, 125; reasons for, 125

Napoleon Complex: application of, 79–80; description of, 79; reference to, 80
National Council of Teachers,, 98

October Sky, 29
Olmos, Edward James. *See Stand and Deliver*

Palmer, Brian, 154
parent/teacher divide, 127–129
Pasternik, Mr., 132
Persall Steve, 14
Philibosian, Robert, 155
Pianta, Dennis, 50–51
Popham, James W., 69
poverty: causes of, 137–138; effects of, 137, 142; fatherlessness, 138, 142; sectionalism, 139
presumption of innocence: and the courts, 154; definition of, 154; reference to, 158, 160
property values, per test scores, 143–144

quality of schools, 143

Ramsey, Harton, 60–61
Ratzfield, Rooney, 140
Restock, Potter, 83
restorative justice: definition of, vii; teachers' reaction to, vii
Rhee, Michelle, 9
Riches, Jim, 71
Rivera, Miss, 87–88
Rubin, Lael, 155–156

Sachs, Wayne, 156
safe zones, 149–150
salary structure. *See* compensation
Sandburg, Carl, 97
Sanders, William David, 133
Sandy Hook Elementary School, 133
scapegoats, teachers as, 161–162
school choice, 92, 151
sensationalism: description of, 160; examples of, 160
sex predators: accusations of, 162–164; cases of, 157–164; commentaries on, 159–160; defense of, 164
Singer, Oscar Allen, 137
shame, 27
Soto, Victoria, 133
Stand and Deliver, 6, 8
status of teachers: description of, 22; rankings, 22–23
Sturgeon, Potter, 26
styles of teaching, 98–100
suicide rates, 25, 34

Teachers: description of, 17; are crazy, 17
technology: challenges of, 3, 10, 107; reference to, 30
testing: anxiety, 59, 60–61; AP/Honors, 57–58, 68; cheating on, 67; containment of, 87; different kinds of, 55, 58; disadvantages of, 64–65; goals of, 67–69; overtesting, 57–58; perplexities about, 62–63; private schools, philosophy of, 58; real-estate values, effect on, 59–60; teachers' comments about, 61–62; varieties of, 63–64; waste of time, 61–62
talents of teachers, 79
tenure: due process as, 45–46, 47; California in, 50; changes in, 48–49, 51; clarifications of, 46, 51–52; description of, 44, 45; perceptions of, 44–45, 47–48
To Kill a Mockingbird, 25
To Sir With Love: description of, 1; reference to, 4
Toussaint, Allen, on "Working in a Coal Mine", 34
training: courses of, 114–115; description of, 114; student teaching, 115
Treu, Rolf, 50

unions: agency fee, 29; benefits of, 39, 40, 71; criticisms of, 71, 72; drawbacks of, 39–40; dues, unfairness of, 86–87; reference to, 12, 151

Van Roekel, Dennis, of the N.E.A., 50–51
vouchers. *See* school choice

Waiting for Superman: awards earned, 8; critiques of, 5; references to, 9–10, 11, 63, 93, 136
Weingarten, Randi, 50
Wegmeyer, Cedrick, 141
Whitman, Walt, 97–98
Williams, Joe, 13
workshops for teachers, xiv

About the Author

Bruce J. Gevirtzman is a retired high school English teacher. He currently teaches part-time at California State University, Fullerton. Bruce is the author of three other books: *Shaking Hands with Aliens: An Intimate Understanding of America's Teenagers*; *Straight Talk to Teachers: Twenty Insane Ideas for a Better Classroom*; and *Audacious Cures for America's Ailing Schools*. He lives with his wife and two teenage children in Brea, California.

www.ingramcontent.com/pod-product-compliance
Lightning Source LLC
Chambersburg PA
CBHW030113010526
44116CB00005B/223